P9-DGH-637

Robert J. Goldstein, Ph.D.

Bettas

Everything About Selection, Care, Nutrition, Behavior, and Training

BARRON'S

2 CONTENTS

INTRODUCTION

The Siamese fighting fish (Betta splendens) belongs to the Anabantoids, Asian and African fishes with a unique breathing organ in the head called a labyrinth.

The labyrinth enables them to breathe air when the water is stagnant. The labyrinth enabled the first tropical aquarium fish, the paradise fish (*Macropodus opercularis*), to survive the boat trip of many weeks from Asia to Europe. The fighting fish, with the same organ, arrived soon after and is today one of the world's most popular tropical fishes.

Labyrinth fishes can swallow air and use its oxygen. Fresh water might hold oxygen at up to 8 parts per million (ppm). Air is 21 percent oxygen or 2,100 ppm, so the worst air is better than the best water. Swamp water might have only 2–3 ppm oxygen. The labyrinth enables anabantoids to survive oxygen-deficient water by swallowing air, while other fishes die of anoxia.

Betta splendens, the Siamese fighting fish, is native to Vietnam, Thailand, Laos, and Cambodia. About a hundred other species of *Betta* occur throughout southern Asia, half now in the hobby, and more imported every year. Most of the newest (and introduced) species of *Betta* are native to the Malay Peninsula and the

White cellophane Betta.

Sunda Islands (Sumatra, Bali, Java, and Borneo). The Anabantoid fishes, including the bettas, gouramies, bushfish, and their relatives, range from southern China throughout Malaysia and Indonesia and into southern Africa.

Fighting Strains

Gambling on fish fights is popular throughout Asia. Two well-matched males are placed in a square glass jar, and the winner is the fish that continues attacking after the other has given up.

Over the centuries (and perhaps millennia), today's fighting fish has been bred to be larger and more robust, with a larger head and jaws. Thai breeders also bred them for colors and finnage and that brought them into the aquarium hobby.

In Thailand, the fish called Pla Kat or biting fish usually indicates *Betta splendens*. A more general term, Pla Kat Par, which refers to all the types of fighting fish found in the wild, is used for *B. splendens*, *B. imbellis*, and *B. smaragdina*. Wild fish from flooded rice fields, ditches, back-waters, and marshes are called

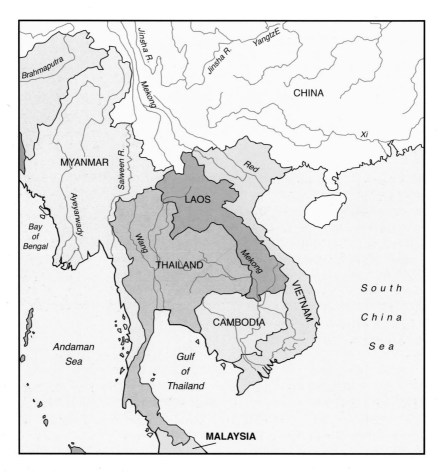

Pla Kat Tung, which means wild biting fish from fields. Domestic fighting strains, Pla Kat Mor, are bred in clay pots.

A fight between two wild male Pla Kat Tung collected from a swamp might last only 15 minutes. A fight between two male Pla Kat Mor lasts up to six hours.

All Pla Kat Mor are short-finned with rounded tails, large bodies, a large head, large upturned jaws with upper and lower lips meeting at the same level, and wide caudal peduncles (that part of the body at the base of the tail fin). The best fighters fall into three categories: *Hakmokwai*—gray-blue/green body with no red in the unpaired fins, and with black pelvic fins; *Angchae*—completely green body with the unpaired fins half red; and *Honkamten*—brown body with rows of green spots and an *imbellis* pattern (crescent) in the tail fin.

Fighting attitude, like physical features, can be inherited. Unlike coloration, there is no way to "see" fighting ability in the offspring, so colors are used as tags for the parental stock. By following the colors of the offspring, the breeders can determine which parent provided the better genes for fighting ability. (If both parents were the same color, the breeders could not tell which offspring carried the better genes for fighting.)

How the fighters are selected for fighting and breeding is a uniquely Thai story.

A male of a good fighting lineage of one color is bred with a female of an unrelated good fighting lineage of another color. A few young fish are fought to see if one color from this cross is associated with superior fighting ability. All the fish of the losing color are discarded. The largest and strongest individuals of the winning color are saved for important, high-stakes fights. Because the fish fight only once, there is constant demand for new and better fighters.

Beautiful Strains

The Thai call veiltail forms Pla Kat Cheen or fish with a Chinese-style silk robe. Cheen indicates long fins and iridescence (sheen). Wild males have slightly elongated dorsal and anal fins, but nothing like the development of the fins in Pla Kat Cheen.

History

In 1850 the ichthyologist Kantor described what he believed to be a variant of the previously known *Betta pugnax*, unaware that he was looking at a new species. Kantor's fish was sent to aquarists in France in 1874, but it would be 19 years before it was spawned by

Super delta.

the Frenchman Jeunet. In 1896 the Germans also succeeded.

In 1909 the American C. Tate Regan recognized and redescribed the fighting fish and named it *Betta splendens*, the splendid betta. By 1910 it was widely bred in Europe and sent to the United States. In 1927 a shipment imported into San Francisco from Thailand included a semi-albino thought to be a different species and named *Betta cambodia*, but later recognized as only a color variety. The name Cambodia is retained today for the semi-albino with a white body and pigmented fins and eyes. Today, selective breeding of *Betta splendens* has given us new colors and color combinations, new kinds of finnage, and a host of new beautiful varieties. Equally dramatic are the advances in bigger and better fighting strains.

Fancy Bettas Gallery

Red Cambodia female.

Blue and orange crowntail.

Blue longfin.

Red female fringe-fin.

Red on Cambodia half moon.

Blue half moon.

Light blue male with red edge fringe.

Iridescent green shortfin male.

Silver and red half moon.

Blue crowntail with red fins.

CHARACTERISTICS OF THE GENUS

The Anabantoidea contains families and subfamilies based, in part, on the shape of the labyrinth. The subfamilies contain genera (plural for genus), each with one or more species.

In older books, you will see *Betta* located in the family Belontiidae, but today it is placed in the family Osphronemidae, based on studies by Britz merging the families Belontiidae, Luciocephalidae (pikeheads), and Osphronemidae. Richter (1981) proposed *"Pseudobetta"* for the mouthbrooding species because they behave differently and some have robust bodies and large heads. His suggestion has no merit.

Breeding Behavior and Fighting Displays

Breeding and fighting are triggered by actions, chemicals, and markings that "release" those behaviors. A pheromone, a chemical hormone released from the body, may release spawning behavior in a fish of the opposite sex. Red and black colors of the stiff branchiostegal membranes beneath the gill covers are releasers

Giant King male Plakat.

of threat behavior in bettas. Another behavioral releaser is undulating the body.

Male anabantoids other than bettas can be induced to fight if isolated a few weeks in a small container. The paradise fish, *Macropodus opercularis*, is trained as a fighting fish in China through just this manipulation.

Fighting fish males become aggressive when confronted with another male or even their own images. In its lateral display, the male erects its unpaired fins and undulates rapidly. In fishes other than fighting fish, this is termed "tail-beating." Threatening males also erect the gill covers (opercula) and spread the underlying branchiostegal membrane, a red plate with a black central band, while facing directly toward the competitor. Other fishes expand their front profiles by gaping the gill covers, but none does it to the degree seen in fighting fish. This is another reason why they are favorites of behavioral scientists (ethologists).

Males also display the same manner to females entering their territory. These displays may be fol-

Finnage

The wild Pla Kat Tung has short fins, with the anal fin markedly extended and pointed in the male compared with the female. The veiltail betta was developed before the first bettas were exported to the West. It probably was developed in Thailand concurrently with cornflower blue, the first color variety.

The male veiltail betta has elongated rays and interconnected membranes of the dorsal, caudal, and anal fins. The extension ranges up to four times normal length, and only males develop this characteristic. The pectoral and pelvic fins are not extended, but are identical to the wild type. The veiltail is probably a single gene mutation.

A second mutation, not sex limited, is the doubletail gene. This mutant has increased fin rays, the final number variable. The extra rays in the caudal fin are bunched above the normal complement and appear as a second tail above the first rather than side by side as in fantail goldfish. This mutation may also manifest as increased dorsal fin rays.

A third mutation is the fringed or combtail betta in which fin rays protrude beyond the limits of the membranes of the unpaired fins, most markedly in the anal and caudal fins. It is not clear whether the rays are programmed to grow beyond the intervening membranes or the membranes cannot keep up with ray growth.

These mutations are inherited independently, and it is possible to have any combination of characters.

lowed by biting the fins, jaws, or bodies of other males or females not willing to spawn.

These aggressive or agonistic behaviors continue to be studied with mirrors, models, and even computerized animations. So far, they suggest that the size of the fish, the size of the flaring gills, and the size of the fins have no effect on the degree of the behavior. From aquarium experiences, it seems the most important influencer of agonistic behavior is whether the fish has been kept in isolation.

Fancy Strains

Betta varieties have increased exponentially since those early days of blue, red, green, and cambodia (white) bettas with single veil tails. Today, bettas are produced in all shades of solid colors, half colors (butterfly), and piebald or marbling.

They may have round tails, veil tails, single tails, double tails, or fringed tails. They can be iridescent all over, iridescent on part of the body, or matte (not iridescent at all).

Colors

The few basic color forms in bettas may be derived from several pathways. That means that two red strains or two yellow or black strains may have entirely different origins. Selective breeding can provide clues to the pathways of any particular strain. But two or more similarly colored strains may have different origins, and when bred to one another generate not the same color as the parents, but the wild type betta.

Color is controlled by chromatophores (pigment cells) in the dermis or deep skin and in the eyes. Many are in cells (melanocytes) that make melanin. Other chromatophores called xanthophores contain xanthins, yellow pigments derived from fats and other compounds derived from carotenoids similar to vitamin A. Another chromatophore is the erythrophore, containing mostly red pigments called pterins, and sometimes other substances. There are about four kinds of chromatophores and four

Air Breathing

Anabantoids evolved during the Devonian Era or Age of Fishes some 60 million years ago. Many fishes have capillaries both in the gill filaments and also on the inside of the gill cover. The ancestors of the anabantoid fishes went one better. In most fishes, the gill arch is a simple bone upon which the gill filaments are located. The anabantoid's gill arch closest to the mouth (the first arch) also developed its own capillaries (vascularized). Over time, the more arch bone that could be vascularized, the more efficient this supplemental oxygen-gathering system. It's a great idea, but there's not much room in a fish's throat. The anabantoid gill arch had little room to expand and instead turned on itself

and convoluted to fit into the gill chamber. With time, this convoluted (labyrinthine) gill arch with its dense capillary tissue became as important as the gills and gill cover filaments and enabled anabantoids to exploit swamps unsuitable for other fishes.

Modern anabantoids vary in the complexity of the labyrinth. It is most convoluted in snakeheads and large gouramies, and least convoluted in bettas, where it is little more than a hollow tube and sac. Dr. Gene Lucas has published photomicrographs showing that the labyrinth might even be connected to the swim bladder, which would complement its otherwise reduced surface area (lacking convolutions).

classes of basic pigments. The combination of pigments and their interactions is responsible for all the betta colors. Any pigment carrier (erythrophore, melanophore, xanthophore) may contain a mix of pigments.

Iridescence

Bettas deposit waste products of nitrogen metabolism in their skin, eyes, and fins. These wastes or guanines are polymers of ammonia. They usually exist as crystalline arrays that refract light and give the fish an iridescent sheen. Crystalline guanine occurs in structures called iridocytes.

Wild bettas have iridocytes in the upper body and fins. Domesticated bettas have been bred to spread them onto the head. The thickness and arrangement of the crystals and the underlying pigments determine whether the fish is some shade of blue to green.

A mutant form deposits the guanine in granular packets in the skin rather than in iridocytes, and these granules do not glisten because they are not crystals. Such fish appear opaque and milky. The deposits can enhance other body colors in domestic bettas, but when the deposits extend to the eyes they cause vision impairment.

Melanin

Black or brown melanin is the most important animal pigment. It is derived from the amino acid alanine, one of the building blocks of proteins. In the body, our cells modify alanine to make other substances. One modification is the addition of a ring called a phenyl group to make a new substance called phenylalanine, another amino acid.

Chemical reactions in the body are mediated by enzymes assisted by molecules called cofactors. Cofactors contain a vitamin such as, for example, folic acid.

Using certain enzymes (mixed function oxidases), phenylalanine is converted to tyrosine (hydroxyphenylalanine). Tyrosine is used in many ways, but most importantly in its conversion to DOPA (dihydroxy-phenylalanine). DOPA can treat Parkinson's disease, and is important to nerve impulse transmission. The conversion of tyrosine to DOPA is mediated by the enzyme tyrosinase. A lack of tyrosinase causes Parkinson's symptoms because DOPA cannot be made from tyrosine. But DOPA is used elsewhere as well.

Much of the alanine and phenylalanine in fish that ends up as DOPA occurs not in nerve cells but in melanocytes. If the fish cannot make tyrosinase, it cannot make melanin and the animal is an albino. The lack of this one substance (tyrosinase) in the brain can cause trembling and in the skin can cause albinism.

In the melanocytes, DOPA is altered to DOPA-quinone, a red pigment. DOPA quinone is unstable and changes to indole quinone, another pigment. Indole quinone combines with itself forming a polymer called melanin. It finally combines with a protein and is now called a melanoprotein. The melanoproteins we see in fish are black and brown pigments (black when oxidized, brown when reduced).

Breeders who have struggled to get a pure black betta, only to end up with a brown fish, may have already succeeded genetically. Getting more melanin into the fish won't make it black. What they need to do is find a way to oxidize the melanin. The key to getting the brown fish to darken to black might be dietary or even temperature-related, as in Siamese cats. At least two kinds of black bettas are

Tyrosine → 3,4-Dihydroxydiphenyl-alanine (DOPA) → Dopa quinone

5,6-Dihydroxydihydro-indole-α-carboxylic acid → Dopa chrone

5,6-Dihydroxyindole → Indole 5,6-quinone

Dopa melanin

common. "Smoky" bettas have a diffuse black pigment. They breed true, and perhaps could be line bred to increase the oxidized melanin.

A different (and older) mutation resulted in black fish that could not be line bred. The offspring from a black male and black female would die almost at once. But a black male bred with a female carrying the black gene but not black herself (half black genetically) resulted in survival of some young.

Perhaps black · black embryos die because putting so much DOPA into melanin deprives the body of DOPA for thyroid function, brain function, hormones and neurotransmitters, and those offspring simply cannot survive.

Then how do we explain a charcoal black betta that is not lethal? For the same reason that when we cross the charcoal betta to a black betta we get a wild-colored (blue-red) betta. The mutations for black and charcoal may be on different loci. When the fish are mated, each recessive mutant gene is masked by a dominant wild-type gene. The offspring carry those recessive genes, but they do not manifest until the next generation of brother-sister matings.

Steel blue iridescence over the black is acceptable to judges, but blue or green iridescence is a disqualifying trait. New varieties include black cambodias, orange fish with black fins, and half moon black bettas.

Carotenoids

Yellow may be caused by carotenoid pigments in xanthophores, or may be an intermediate in the production of melanin. Many fishes throw yellow (xanthic) sports in nature. The most common cause is interrupted melanin formation from a deficiency of tyrosinase. The complete absence of tyrosinase in melanocytes (but not in brain) could lead to albinism while its partial absence could lead to yellow or red, both pre-melanin conditions. A complete loss of DOPA everywhere in the body would, of course, be a lethal mutation. Yellow colors are possible through the melanin pathway, the xanthin pathways for carotenoids, or the pterin pathways for cofactors like folic acid. Different yellow strains may have different causes.

Pterins

Red might result from interrupted melanin formation, but that seems unlikely in bettas. We know another kind of red can result from the pathway leading to astaxanthin. Red can also result from pterin pigments in bettas, platies, swordtails, and fruit flies. Pterins occur in structures called pterinosomes, and are made of chemicals called pteridines, quite similar to guanine. We already noted that guanine in skin is a waste product of nitrogen metabolism. It's also a building block of DNA, so where it occurs and its structure determine its value. Katherine Royal, a student of Dr. Gene Lucas, showed in the 1970s that red in *Betta splendens* is caused by pterins and carotenoids like astaxanthin and that at least two (and probably more) strains of red betta differ in their concentrations of pterins and astaxanthin.

What's the point of red colors in bettas or any other fishes? In fact, red isn't the point. Pterins are cofactors for waste product metabolism regulated by the enzyme xanthine oxidase. Pterins inhibit the enzyme and the production of waste uric acid. The red pigment is nothing more than a byproduct of metabolism.

Pterin

Xanthopterin
(2-amino-4,6-dihydroxy pteridine)

Summary

The adult pigment cells are derived from a type of embryonic cell that can develop several ways. Melanophores contain melanoprotein that can be yellow, brown, or black, and might carry carotenoids. Pterinosomes formed in the embryo can carry red, yellow, or orange. Xanthophores can contain xanthins (yellow pigments), carotenoids (yellow, orange, or red), pterins (red, yellow, or orange), or a combination of pigments. Separate erythrophores might contain additional red, yellow, or black pigments. The pathways result in different colors if they lack a single enzyme in a series. Domestic betta colors are caused by combinations of mutations in these pathways.

Today we have the laboratory tools to isolate genes from one animal, insert them into harmless viruses, and use those viruses to deliver the genes to another animal's embryo. We found genes we didn't know existed, genes that were metabolically turned off in the past, but lend themselves to being switched back on. The variations and colors of domestic bettas will be far different 20 years from now.

Judging Bettas

The most important considerations in judging bettas are body and fin proportions. Think of a betta show as you would a human beauty contest, where grace, style, and proportion are more important than height, long hair, or the swimsuit competition.

The International Betta Congress (IBC) training program for certified judges includes seminars, experience, videos, a two-year apprenticeship under a certified judge, continuing education, and evaluations by peers. Judges are expected to adhere to standards and guidelines, but allowed latitude in aesthetics.

The IBC holds several shows a year in different regions such as the American southeastern states, western states, and internationally. Show categories include males and females of many strains, wild fish, species related to *B. splendens*, and even photography, drawings, and arts and crafts.

The IBC handbook describes ideal form and color for different categories. The body of a male should be at least 1.5 inches long with a shorter length cause for disqualification, and neither too sleek nor too robust. A female should have the ideal wild-type female shape, and be smaller than the ideal male. Giant females are not rewarded for giantism, nor are females with male characteristics, and such fish

may be disqualified. The body should be free of blemishes and diseases.

Doubletail, single tail, and short-finned types are judged separately. A veiltail male should have a dorsal fin equal in size to the anal fin, a symmetrical anal fin not much longer in the rear than in the front, a symmetrical caudal fin expanded equally in all dimensions rather than so heavy it drops toward the bottom, and fin lengths (measured from the middle of the base of the fin to the outer edge along a center ray) about one half the length of the body. A betta with unusually long or large fins is not desirable because it is not proportional.

The most common faults for which points are lost are extra fin rays, bent rays, and tails

Sex Determination in Bettas

In school we learned that sex determination is based on the XX, XY chromosome model where one pair of chromosomes in the male is unequal and called the XY or male pair; the corresponding equal or XX condition is considered the female sex chromosomes. Many fish have quite different sex determination systems. In some, none of the chromosome pairs are unequal, and in others sex is determined by multiple pairs of chromosomes. In many fish, the sexes are determined through environmental conditions such as age of the parents or pH of the water. In still others, all individuals develop into a male first, later transforming into a female, and in yet others the reverse sequence occurs. There is even one fish that is a combination male and female, laying fertilized eggs all by itself.

There are no unequal chromosomes in bettas that might be sex chromosomes. However bettas seem to follow the XX, XY model since they normally produce 50 percent of each sex. Bettas can produce surprises. If young males are bred with old females, the resulting offspring are mostly males. If the fry are held at abnormal conditions during the first 6 weeks, an overwhelming percentage of males is again produced. And if females are partially ovariectomized (most of their ovaries cut away), they transform into fully functional males (Lucas, 1983).

not perfectly symmetrical. Doubletails must show a deep separation between the two lobes arising from the caudal peduncle, and this, too, is difficult to achieve. Doubletails with a long-based dorsal fin must meet standards for equivalence in size with the anal fin (it is smaller than the anal in veiltails).

Colors of the body and fins are judged separately for richness, evenness, location or margins (as in butterfly bettas), and purity (no other colors showing through). Black is difficult to judge, but a sheen of blue or green is undesirable. Iridescence is also difficult to judge because it is affected by the angle of reflected light and underlying pigments.

There are no points awarded for innovative crosses resulting in unusual genotypes. What the judges see is what the fish is worth in points, irrespective of how difficult the task of producing that betta.

BUBBLENESTING BETTAS

The seminal study that placed the species of Betta into taxonomic groups is that of Witte and Schmidt (1992). In this chapter and the next, Witte and Schmidt's organization and species groups will be explained, and the members of each group described and discussed.

New species of *Betta* are frequently discovered and named in a scientific journal (sometimes in an aquarium publication), and simultaneously made available to the aquarium hobby through specialized clubs or personal contacts. During the past three decades, Swiss, Singaporean, and German scientists and aquarists have introduced new species to the hobby. Notable are Frank Schäfer, Horst Linke, H. J. Richter, H. Pinter, Jorge Vierke, Maurice Kottelat, Kai-Erik Witte, P. K. L. Ng, Tan Heok Hui, Ingo Schindler, Jurgen Schmidt, Tan Swee Hee, Walter Foersch, and Dieter Schaller.

As Dr. Kottelat states, we are still in a discovery phase of the genus *Betta*, with more than half the species discovered and described within the past 25 years.

Betta species are widely distributed over Malaysia, Indonesia, Thailand, Cambodia, and other islands and states. One of the largest and richest areas for new, beautiful species is the state of Kalimantan, making up most of the island of Borneo.

Bubblenesters

Most bubblenesting species come from still waters, with temperatures from 75°F/24°C to 95°F/35°C, the water stained by peat and dead leaves, acidic pH in the range of 4–5.5, low to moderate dissolved calcium hardness, and low conductivity indicating few salts or calcium ions in the water. In these ditches, swamps, river backwaters, floodplains, rice paddies, and canals, the bottom is often mud and silt, the water is less than two feet deep, and the fish occur in dense vegetation. They may be at the shoreline or in vegetated areas in deeper water. The heat and humidity of the air are stifling. Under these conditions, bubblenests provide the eggs and prolarvae antimicrobial, protective mucus from the male parent, and support that maintains eggs and fry near the surface

*A Betta **bubblenest**.*

film where dissolved oxygen concentrations are highest. At this time, the young have not yet developed gills or the labyrinth, and oxygen (richest at the surface film) is absorbed directly through body tissues.

The following conditions will probably apply to most new bubblenesting bettas. The following are minimal conditions for bubblenesting bettas 2 to 3 inches long. Scale up as needed. First, have a tight-fitting cover for the tank.

Betta smaragdina.

House a pair in a 5- to 10-gallon aquarium with dechlorinated and aged (let the bubbles disappear) tap water. A common spawning trigger is a large water change with softened water (deionized, reverse osmosis, rainwater, or even supermarket gallons of softened water for steam irons). Add one teaspoon of non-iodized table salt per five gallons of water to offset the stress of metabolic ammonia and nitrites while maintaining water softness (lack of calcium hardness). As with *B. splendens,* sexes should be conditioned separately on live foods, supplemented with frozen foods, and the female should be introduced gradually to the male either in an adjacent glass compartment or by providing a refugium of dense vegetation. For her safety, the female should be removed after spawning. The male should be removed when the fry can reach the surface unassisted.

Cover the tank to prevent startled fish from leaping out, to retain humidity during labyrinth development, to exclude airborne dust and oils that interfere with oxygen exchange, and to buffer the surface water temperature from room temperature by providing a dead air space.

Newly hatched bubblenester fry should be fed infusoria (rotifers or ciliates) for three weeks, with newly hatched brine shrimp added after the first week. As the young fish grow, they should be sorted by size to minimize cannibalism and the effects of growth inhibiting substances.

The tanks should have floating and submersed vegetation to provide hiding places for the female, and for support of a bubblenest. In cold months, use a low wattage heater and thermometer adjusted to about 85°F (30°C) and inspected daily for unacceptable deviations. These should be dealt with by changing heaters rather than resetting thermostats. With these preparations, you are ready to try your hand at obtaining and breeding bubblenesters.

Several newer species are known or suspected to be bubblenesters, based on breeding reports, relationships, or even appearance. In the following accounts, I have tried to treat taxonomically related fishes together in species groups. Some species are not members of any group and are treated separately.

Splendens Group

There are at least five species in the *B. splendens* species group (*B. splendens*, *B. imbellis*, *B. stiktos*, *B. smaragdina*, and *B. rubra*). The group is not well defined, mostly because Pla Kat enthusiasts from throughout Southeast Asia trade and release fish, cross strains that might be species, and fail to cross others.

Betta stiktos TAN AND NG, 2005 is a recently described member of the *B. splendens* species

Betta stiktos *from Stung Treng, Cambodia.*

group from the upper Mekong River basin of Cambodia. Its distinguishing characters are five rows of black spots in the dorsal fin, fewer than 10 black bands on the caudal fin, and black-speckled scales on the body. Not generally available to the hobby, it is little known.

We know where the newly described species were found, but not their full range, nor the

Imbellis and Splendens— Are They the Same?

Betta splendens was the second tropical fish that started the home aquarium hobby, right behind the paradise fish *(Macropodus)*. The fish called *Betta imbellis* is either a variant or a distinct species. In repeated trials, Dr. Gene Lucas crossed wild *B. imbellis* with domestic *B. splendens* carrying mutations for color and finnage. In all cases the offspring carried the genes of both parents and themselves were fertile, suggesting they're one and the same species. This is powerful evidence that *B. imbellis* is the same species as *B. splendens*, and that the name *B. imbellis* should be discarded.

Betta imbellis.

full historic range of *B. splendens*. The differences among the species seem reliable and, for that reason, all the names presented in this book are accepted at face value until shown otherwise by new data based on DNA analyses.

The fish called *B. imbellis* LADIGES, 1975 is native to Penang Island in Malaysia, western Borneo, and Sumatra. A population at Ko Samui Island off Thailand is endangered. The natural habitat includes swamps, paddies, ditches, canals, and flooded waterways that may reach more than 90°F (32°C). Not exceeding 2 inches in total length, *B. imbellis* is dark blue with bright red pelvic fins, red in the rear of the anal fin, and blue or green double bars on the gill cover. The red crescent in the rear of the caudal fin illustrated in many publications is not diagnostic, as it occurs in both *B. imbellis* and wild *B. splendens*. The male of *B. imbellis* has iridescent blue or green double bars on the gill cover. *B. imbellis* is bred for fighting (short fins) and for beauty

(long finnage), but has not been as extensively developed as *B. splendens* fancy strains. It is reputed to be a faster and more unpredictable attacker than *B. splendens*.

Linke reports that fish grown together get along, and fighting occurs when fish raised separately are placed together, as in *B. splendens*. Otherwise, a group can be held in a single tank where pairs spawn separately beneath submersed or emersed structures, including floating plants. The parents do not prey on the young, but a better yield will result if they are removed. Linke started the fry on TetraMikroMin, a prepared powdered food. Pinter had them breed at 10-day intervals for four or five episodes, with 80–150 eggs per spawning. The fry were started on infusoria (rotifers and ciliates) and easily raised. Populations imported have been named (Donoso, 1989) blue M1, Sungei Semberong, Slim River, Kuantan, Ko Samui, and Penang. The fry grow rapidly, but are sensitive to changes in water quality, and may be killed by water change. Therefore, first remove old water, and then replace the water by dripping it from an overhead reservoir through partly clamped airline tubing.

B. smaragdina LADIGES, 1972 resembles *B. imbellis* but lacks a red crescent in the caudal fin. Prominent are the rows of green or blue iridescent scales on the flank, iridescence on the gill covers, and green and red finnage. The overall impression is "bejeweled." It occurs in marshes, rice paddies, ditches, and floodplains of the Mekong River basin of Thailand, Cambodia, Vietnam, and Laos, and is most common near Nong Khai, near Vientiane, Laos, on the Korat Plateau in northeast Thailand. This fish attains 3 inches/7½ cm total length. *B. sma-*

Betta rubra *from Aceh, Sumatra.*

ragdina has been line bred for the fighting and gambling market (short fins) and for the aquarium display market (long finnage). The most aggressive fish are from Udon Thani, a province south of Nong Khai province, in the northern part of the Korat Plateau in north-eastern Thailand. It breeds readily in soft, warm water in densely vegetated aquariums. A tank can contain several females with one male, should be densely vegetated, and water quality should approximate 8-10 dH hardness, pH 6.5–7.0, and temperature of 75–82°F/24–28°C. This bubblenester accepts caves (flower pots, coconut shells), but will spawn beneath vegetation, and is peaceful when breeding if the female is receptive. If she is not ready, he may kill her, and hiding places are important to her survival. Eggs number about 100–150 and hatch in 30 hours at 77°F/25°C. After three days the fry are free swimming. At this time the male should be removed and feedings of infusoria and microworms started. After four days you can begin feeding newly hatched brine shrimp. Ken Muller reported that in well-planted tanks, this fish won't pursue and eat fry after they begin

taking brine shrimp nauplii. Maturity is reached at six months.

Almost from its original importation, difficulties with abnormal sex ratios and spawning successes induced several betta experts, including scientists, to hybridize the fish with *B. splendens* (Liebetrau, 1982). As a result, any domestic *B. smaragdina* in the hobby may be hybrids.

Betta smaragdina.

Bellica Group

Betta bellica represents a group of at least two species (*B. bellica* and *B. simorum*) characterized by large size (4 to 5 inches), elongated central filaments in the caudal fin, and a distribution including Malaysia and northeastern Sumatra.

Betta bellica SAUVAGE, 1884 was originally reported from Perak, Malaysia, and redescribed in 1996 by Tan and Ng. They determined that *B. fasciata* from Deli (Medan), Sumatra, is a synonym. *B. bellica* now has a known distribution including Terengganu, Perak, Selangor, Pahang, and Johor (and possibly Muar) in peninsular Malaysia and near Medan in Sumatra.

Betta bellica.

Betta simorum *from Jambi, Sumatra, Indonesia.*

All habitats for *B. bellica* are blackwater streams or acid waters associated with peat swamp forests, where it feeds mostly on dragonfly nymphs. Associates in different parts of its range include *B. tussyae, B. waseri, B. hipposideros, B. livida, B. imbellis, B. persephone*, and *B.* cf. *pugnax*. It is the largest bubblenesting betta (more than 3 inches in body length alone and robust), and is not easy to breed in captivity.

   B. bellica is brown with green iridescent scales, more prominent in the males who also have longer unpaired fins. A recently imported purple iridescent fish is called *B. bellica* from Muar, Malaysia.

   Betta simorum TAN AND NG, 1996 occurs in peat swamps draining into the Batang Hari and Indragiri rivers in Jambi and Riau provinces in central eastern Sumatra. These blackwater habitats are shallows among thick leaf litter and below overhanging vegetation, in stagnant to slowly flowing waters. Associates include *B. coccina, B.* cf. *fusca, B. renata, Parosphromenus sumatranus, Belontia hasselti, Trichogaster leeri*, and *Sphaerichthys osphromenoides. B simorum* differs from *B. bellica* in scale and fin ray counts. *B. simorum* has a slightly smaller head than *B. bellica*. It has iridescent green scales as in *B. bellica*, but its protruding central caudal fin rays are longer.

Coccina Group

   Betta coccina represents a group of slender, elongate species, often deep red with a blue-green blotch on the middle of the flank in one sex (*B. coccina, B. uberis*) or both sexes (*B. livida, B. brownorum*) or not at all (*B. rutilans, B. persephone, B. miniopinna, B. tussyae,*

Betta simorum.

B. burdigala). The gill covers sometimes have red or (occasionally) yellow bars. They all have eight or nine abdominal vertebrae (vs. 10 or 11 in other species of *Betta*), and all occur in shallow, acidic, black waters of peat forest flood plains, which have been called semi-aquatic ecotopes. When Vierke discovered *B. coccina* only three decades ago, he had no idea of the number of related species that subsequently would be described by Tan and Tan, Witte and Schmidt, Schaller, Kottelat,

Betta coccina *Sumatra variability.*

and Ng, nor the revolution in *Betta* biology and systematics by Witte and Schmidt that this discovery would stimulate.

The habitat is extreme even for fishes that tolerate low levels of oxygen. These flooded peat forest floors may have an accumulation of leaf litter 2 inches thick, through which grow *Cryptocoryne* and *Nymphaea* at heights varying in response to the fluctuating water levels as the flood plain is inundated and partially desiccated. Blackwater streams enriched with tannic and humic acids leached from the peat and detritus lower the pH to as low as pH 3.5, with a range of 4-5.5 common.

Betta coccina.

Roads through these forests often have drainage ditches alongside, or slowly flowing, almost stagnant, narrow streams of surprising depth, perhaps even 2 feet or more in midstream. Ponds and wet depressions are common. Most of these habitats are connected to permanent streams and rivers that replenish the ponds with perennial fishes including *Rasbora*, many kinds of anabantoid fishes (especially *Belontia, Anabas, Trichogaster, Trichopsis, Parosphromenus,* and *Helostoma*), and siluroids (catfishes) capable of air-breathing. The small species of the *B. coccina* group feed on terrestrial ants and mites. Unlike other bubblenesters, they remain in family groupings that defend the family territory, at least in aquaria and presumably in the wild. Intermittent mouthbrooding, in response to disturbances, has been reported in *B. rutilans* and in a species similar to *B. brownorum*. It was the coccina group that stimulated the revolutionary study by Witte and Schmidt upon which current *Betta* taxonomy is based. Members of the *B. coccina* group in general do not overlap in distribution, but might represent local geographic variations. However, people who have bred the species have been unable to breed hybrids, so the fish seem, at least, behaviorally isolated.

Betta coccina VIERKE, 1979 is reddish brown to wine red, with an iridescent square green blotch on the middle of the flank in the male. It is reported from Malaysia and Sumatra, but a form from Indonesia that may have been

Betta brownorum *with no spot.*

selectively bred has extended central caudal fin rays. The Malaysian aquarium stock is from Muar, and the Sumatra stock from Jambi. Donoso (1989) provided other locales, and speculated that *B. coccina* occurs only in a small part of the west coast of Malaysia and in Sumatra, whereas the related *B. tussyae* occurs far away on the east coast of Malaysia.

Linke collected it in both clear and black, soft, acidic (pH 4-5) high-quality water. Early importations often died of stress-induced velvet disease (*Piscinoodinium*). Many successful spawnings have been reported, including inside floating black plastic tubes (Boggs, 1983) and under leaves. The fry are usually given infusoria or green water as a first food, but have been raised with brine shrimp nauplii as the first food. Fry are highly susceptible to velvet disease. Tony Pinto reported males aggressive during spawning (he uses five-gallon tanks), but both parents can remain in the tank after breeding and do not eat eggs in the bubblenest nor the fry. He removes the offspring for grow-out after two months. *Betta coccina* lives and breeds to at least three years of age, but fish under a year old produce small spawns.

Donoso (1989) found males aggressive, causing noncompetitive fishes (both sexes) to jump out of the tanks until he finally planted his tanks densely. His first fish were infested with what might have been *Piscinoodinium*, but recovered with high temperature (93°F/34°C), after which the temperature was reduced to 77–84°F/25–29°C. The tap water was treated to be clear, slightly acidic (pH 5.2), soft, and blackened with wood extract. His adult fish took frozen brine shrimp, bloodworms, and mysids, but ignored *Tubifex* worms and *Daphnia*, although they took the small insects

contaminating the wild *Daphnia*. Females developed a bright green horizontal line in breeding mode, and the male's green mark was enhanced by white edging. The fish produced quite small spawns (30–60 eggs yielding perhaps 10 fry) in small (less than 2 inches wide, one or two bubbles deep) bubblenests, and the fry were delicate. He fed Liquifry and powdered food for several weeks, and the fry began to grow after switching to *Artemia* nauplii at almost a month of age. The aged adults became faded and unattractive.

B. livida NG AND KOTTELAT, 1992 is red with a green blotch on the flank (more prominent in males and larger fishes of both sexes but not always apparent) and brilliant red fins. It can be recognized by the green midlateral blotch in both sexes, green tips to the pelvic fins (not white as in *B. brownorum*), two parallel vertical gold bars on the gill cover, and 10 or 11 dorsal fin rays. The body is red, the fins maroon with green streaks. The fish were collected from blackwater streams and pools in a peat forest in north Selangor, on the central west coast of the Malaysian peninsula. Tony Pinto and David

Betta livida.

Betta brownorum.

Armitage collected *B. livida* in the Selangor area north of Johore on the western side of the Malaysian peninsula, north of the localities of *B. coccina*. When the two species were compared side by side, they were quite different. The *B. livida* habitat was low pH (3.5–3.7) and stagnant or slowly flowing tea-colored water, and the fish collected in detritus or leaf litter.

Betta rutilans *wild.*

B. brownorum WITTE AND SCHMIDT, 1992 is a spectacular fish from the Sarawak River basin near Matang and near Kuching and Matang in Sarawak on Borneo. The body is red with a green midlateral blotch in both sexes. It has 10 to 11 dorsal rays, and white lanceolate leading pelvic fin rays. The median (unpaired) fins lack any blue-green spots in front. The iris is iridescent blue. Females are similar to males, but the midlateral green blotch is less pronounced.

Acidic water is required for maintaining the stickiness of the bubblenest, which may be incomplete at the initiation of spawning, but is enlarged afterward. The prolarvae hatch in 36 hours and become free-swimming larvae that begin feeding at 30 hours. Maturity is reached in six months, and maximum size (2 inches) is reached in a year. In response to predators or other disturbances, the male may take the eggs or larvae in his mouth, and move them to another location where he builds a nest. The female normally defends the territory against intruders while the male guards the nest.

Larger fry do not feed on younger siblings, and an entire family of variously aged and sized fish may occupy and defend a small territory. This behavior also applies to *B. persephone*, and may apply to all members of the *B. coccina* group (Schmidt, 1992).

B. rutilans WITTE AND KOTTELAT IN KOTTELAT, 1991 is slender, small, and deep red (both sexes) without a distinctive blotch on the flank. Juveniles are striped. It differs from the quite similar *B. tussyae* in having one rather than two dorsal fin spines, two rather than three anal fin spines. It differs from all *Betta* species in having fused hypural plates number 6 and 7 (bones in the base of the tail). It was collected from streams of the Pinyuh and Kepayang rivers, the latter north of Pontianak, near Anjungan, and in Kalimantan Barat (west Kalimantan) on Borneo. Linke found it in a marshy soft, acidic blackwater stream.

This bubblenester produces about 30 large eggs that hatch into fry larger than those of some mouthbrooders. The prolarvae have yolk sacs and are incapable of swimming. If disturbed, the male takes them or the eggs into his mouth for safekeeping or placement elsewhere. Linke suspected the fish was a mouthbrooder, but it is not. It mouths the eggs to protect them from sudden danger for periods of several days at most. In the bubblenest, the fry constantly fall and are retrieved and returned by the male. Subsequently, the prolarvae leave the bubblenest and hang vertically from an adjacent leaf by their heads, suggesting cement head glands as described by Jones (1940). Cement glands on prolarvae may be more important than bubblenest mucus in providing support.

B. persephone SCHALLER, 1986 reaches only an inch and a half, with a slender brown to blue-black body, blue unpaired fins, and brilliant blue irises. In nuptial coloration, the male is more intensely colored, but otherwise the sexes are similarly colored and quite beautiful. It is closest to *B. miniopinna* from which it usually differs in having black rather than red pelvic

Betta rutilans.

Betta persephone.

Betta persephone.

fins, but this trait is unreliable. It is known from several locales in Malaysia, including Muar. It hides among leaves, roots, and debris in soft, acid water of the river floodplain, and survives low water by finding damp locations beneath leaves.

It is best kept as single pairs in heavily vegetated tanks with R.O. water filtered through peat moss for a pH of about 5.0, and one or two dried oak leaves to assist tannin deposition and maintenance of low pH. Feed live foods only. The male will use a floating tube for refuge and build its nest adjacent. Spawns are small with up to 40 eggs, and the fry initially need infusoria or a dried equivalent (APR or artificial-plankton-rotifer) for a week before they can take brine shrimp nauplii. Fry can be left with the parents and with previous spawns in a family tank, and cannibalism is not evident (Pinto, 2000). Growth is slow with maturity attained in nine months, at which time the males become territorial and aggressive.

B. coccina is reputed to occur together with *B. persephone* in the Muar region, but Tony Pinto and David Armitage were unable to find it, despite searching. Dr. Tan has seen mixed imports from Malaysia containing both *B. coccina* and *B. persephone*, but has yet to personally collect *B. coccina* from the Malaysian peninsula.

B. miniopinna TAN AND TAN, 1994 was collected at Pulau Bintan, an island in the Riau Archipelago, Indonesia. It was found in a swamp forest stream and another stream near a rubber plantation. Conditions were generally shaded, acidic (pH 4.9), tea-colored, shallow water among leaf litter over mud. Associates included two other undescribed species related to (but not) *B. pugnax* and *B. spilotogena*. This elongate, almost black fish with iridescent green dorsal and caudal fins resembles *B. persephone*, but differs by having red rather than black pelvic fins, although both have white tips on these fins. It differs from its rela-

Betta tussyae.

tives in the *B. coccina* species group by fin and scale counts. Both sexes look alike. It is one of the members of the group without a green midlateral blotch.

B. tussyae SCHALLER, 1985 is another red member of this species group that lacks the central flank spot. It was collected at Pahang, near the town of Kuantan in eastern Malay-

Betta burdigala.

sia. It occurs amid dense vegetation and dead leaves in small streams where the water is often soft and acidic (pH 5.5). Populations of *B. tussyae* collected from different locales are known as MK 314, km 310 Mersing-Johor-Baru, and M14+M16 (Donoso, 1989).

B. burdigala KOTTELAT AND NG, 1994 is known only from Banka, 4 kilometers north of Bikang village on the road from Koba to Toboali in Indonesia. The habitat was a peat swamp along the road in a new-growth forest. When collected during high water, the fish were among tree and plant roots in the flooded forest. Like other members of its group, *B. burdigala* (the name is Latin for Bordeaux) is a deep red fish having three dark red stripes on the head. It is the only member of the *B. coccina* group with iridescent green patches on the first third of the dorsal and anal fins. The dorsal fin has a thin white margin. *B. burdigala* has eight or nine abdominal vertebrae vs. 10 or 11 in all other *Betta* species, and a total dorsal fin ray count of 14 or 15 elements *vs.* 10 or 11 in

Betta uberis.

other members of the *B. coccina* group and seven to 11 in all other *Betta* species.

B. uberis TAN AND NG, 2006 has been previously called the *Betta* from Pankalanbun, a location in western Borneo's Arnt River basin. This peat swamp forest dweller is reddish brown, the male darker, the female with a green flush. Males have a green mid-body spot or no spot at all, and green streaks on the unpaired fins.

Wild Bettas Gallery

Betta macrostoma.

Betta pugnax.

Betta foerschi.

Betta albimarginata.

Betta coccina.

Betta brownorum.

Collecting Betta persephone.

The mouthbrooding bettas range from as small as a stunted B. splendens (B. picta) to the largest members of the genus at more than 5 inches, excluding the tail. They differ in many ways from the bubblenesters and are, in general, easier to keep. They must be kept covered, less to protect the developing labyrinth than to keep the adults and juveniles from jumping out of the aquarium.

In general, mouthbrooders occupy flowing rather than stagnant lowland water bodies (streams rather than ponds), with higher-quality water that is close to neutral pH (6.5–7.2), and moderate hardness from calcium-laden bedrock. They are native to upland streams where the slope provides moderate flow, and stream sizes from trickles to rivers often 20 feet wide or greater. Within these (usually) slowly flowing streams and rivers, the mouthbrooders tend to cluster in barely flowing riverbank indentations out of the main current, in backwaters, and in undercut banks where the bottom is typically mixed silt and sand, as opposed to midriver where the bottom often is clean and sandy or littered with rocks. In its nearshore microhabitats, the mouthbrooders are often found in dense vegetation.

Mouthbrooding male **Betta pardalatos** *from Palembang, Sumatra.*

Mouthbrooding in this genus is an adaptation to flowing water, where a bubblenest on the surface could not persist. It enables the fish to breed in the absence of a densely vegetated, quiet shallow environment, converts the male's buccal cavity (throat) into a mobile nest, allows the fry to develop in safety until they are large enough to withstand moderate currents and feed on their own, and enables the parents to deliver the fry to a remote nursery area for release. The safety of the fry from predators is ensured within the buccal cavity of the male. Mouthbrooding also allows adult fish to socialize by eliminating nest territorial defense. It may also be associated with synchronized spawning, as discussed under *Betta picta*.

All the mouthbrooders are peaceful and are not used for fighting in their native countries. Many can be kept in single species communal tanks without danger to either sex. Maintain

Bettas *spawning.*

them in large, covered 20-gallon tanks in moderate to hard water at neutral pH, and not in rainwater. In most locales, dechlorinated tap water is fine for these bettas. They do well on live and frozen foods, and can be fed dry foods because leftover particles do not readily decay and lower pH in hard water as they do in soft water (rainwater).

Provide open space and structure, with rooted plants, overturned flowerpots, rocks, and caves. Use outside filters with carbon to maintain high-quality water. Because most of these fishes are larger than bubblenesters, they can be fed shaved, frozen shrimp and beef

heart and other prepared meats, and regular meals of blackworms, tubifex worms, white worms, and small earthworms. Frequent partial water changes will maintain high water quality and may induce spawning.

Spawning Triggers

There are two modes of spawning. Most of the larger species should be separately conditioned for two weeks on live foods in small quarters, and then placed together in a 10- or 20-gallon covered spawning tank with dense vegetation. Others (for example, *B. picta*) respond to a massive (25 percent) water change with next day simultaneous (group) spawning in the communal tank. Breeding occurs in the open or in a sheltered clearing, close to the bottom or in midwater. Spawning is initiated by the female, and the standard betta embrace occurs with the female wrapped at a right angle within the arched body of the male, their reproductive vents in apposition. The eggs do not fall freely as in bubblenesting bettas, but are gathered or at least slowed in their descent by the curved anal fin of the male, which acts as a cup. Then, as the large, white eggs fall from the male's anal fin, the female recovers, rushes down to intercept the falling eggs, and gathers them in her mouth. As the recovering male joins her, she spits the eggs toward him, and he gathers them for subsequent brooding.

Brooding males should be isolated until the large fry are released seven to 12 days later. After release, the males should be placed back in the communal tank. The fry typically take newly hatched live brine shrimp as a first food, so infusoria culture is not necessary. Clutches range from 20 to 100 depending on the size and experience of the adults.

Betta anabatoides BLEEKER, 1850 is widespread through the southern part of Borneo (Kalimantan). Males may or may not have blue-green iridescent scales and a hint of yellow in the anal fin to distinguish them from females (sometimes this is difficult), females have no bright colors or dark markings, and both sexes may have fringed and even spade-shaped caudal fins. Linke described its habitat as watercourses with low pH (4.8 and below) and quite soft. It was found along banks in dense vegetation. In aquaria it spawns at 75–80°F/24–26.5°C.

Dimidiata Group

The *Betta dimidiata* species group *(B. dimidiata, B. krataios)* are recognized by their small size and the wide blue lower portion (not just the margin) of the anal fin. These dwarf mouthbrooders are native to the Kapuas River basin of Borneo.

Betta dimidiata ROBERTS, 1989 is less than 3 inches body length, with black blotches on a slim, reddish brown body and a broad silver submarginal band on the anal fin. The male has blue highlights in his elongate unpaired fins, extended central rays in the caudal, and becomes deep red in nuptial coloration. Older males may develop fin extensions in captivity. This dwarf mouthbrooder is native to the Kapuas River basin in Borneo. Pinto (1999) kept them in R.O. water filtered through peat and reported high temperatures (78°F/25.5°C)

Betta dimidiata.

Betta krataios.

necessary to maintain good health. At this high temperature (for a mouthbrooder), the fish readily breeds, producing up to 30 minute fry (requiring a week of infusoria) after 12 to 14 days incubation. Growth is slow, and males are aggressive in the absence of roomy quarters and vegetation for hiding places.

Betta krataios TAN AND NG, 2006 is native to the Sangau and Mandor regions of the lower Kapuas River basin in Borneo. This dwarf mouthbrooder sports a broad patch of iridescent blue scales from behind the eye to the edge of the gill cover on the lower half of the cheek, a broad iridescent blue band on most of the outer anal fin, blue pelvic fins, and a red iris. It is stocky, with a black patch below the eye and either four to six dark blotches or vertical bands or three horizontal stripes (according to comfort or fright) along the flank. In captivity it never develops elongated fins.

Betta edithae VIERKE, 1984 is a name that applies solely to one species on the island of Sumatra in Indonesia. Displaying males are reddish brown with iridescent green scale edges forming rows of tiny bright spots. The unpaired fins are richly hued with brown rays and light blue membranes. A black band from the lower lips extends through the eye across the gill cover. Brooding males are light bodied, with three or four black horizontal lines, the

Betta edithae.

second through the eye to the lips, and the unpaired fins remain strikingly patterned. At only 2½ inches (7 cm), *B. edithae* is a small mouthbrooder that can be kept with other small fishes, including rasboras and tetras. Maintain hardness at no more than 10 dH, pH of 7.5 to 6.0, and temperature 77–82°F/25–28°C. It does not need a cave, but will spawn in the open and near the surface. The female is ignored after breeding. At 82°F/28°C, the male will release 20–40 fry after nine days, and the young can take *Artemia* nauplii at once. Frequent feedings and high-quality water (frequent small water changes of 5–10 percent every two days) produce rapid growth, but more massive water changes induce life–threatening skin irritations in the young. Maturity occurs at six months of age.

Betta midas TAN, 2009 is an often yellow-gold or xanthic fish restricted to Borneo, previously (and incorrectly) known in the hobby as "*Betta edithae* from Pontianak," a location in Borneo. The yellow color is exhibited by adapted fish, but isn't apparent in stressed fish.

Betta macrostoma REGAN, 1909 is reddish brown on the body and fins, with variable black pigment below the eye and on at least the lower half of the gill cover, the two black areas converging at the throat, and emphasized by black rays in the pectoral fins. The male is more intensely pigmented. His anal fin usually has a broad black margin, and there may be a lighter edge. His dorsal fin has a thin, white margin and a black spot not quite an ocellus at the rear, whereas the female lacks the black mark in this fin. The male's caudal fin has a thin white margin, a broad black submargin, and two or three broad vertical black bands separated by light areas, whereas the

Betta macrostoma.

female's caudal fin has only the dark margin and sometimes a peduncular spot. Juveniles have two rows of spots on the body. This large, 5-inch fish is found in soft, acid water (pH 4.3), but reproducing those conditions in captivity is stressful and the fish readily falls victim to bacterial infections. Linke noted that the young are large when released at 20 days of age, and readily take *Artemia* nauplii. The adults require a varied diet rich in live insects. Robert Nhan reported them difficult to keep, and fed his fish with live adult *Artemia* and *Drosophila*, plus other live foods. Pinter reported the fish from cool, running water, but that is probably an error in light of Linke's highly detailed report. There do not appear to be any closely related species.

Betta schalleri KOTTELAT AND NG, 1994 was described from many locations in Bangka, Indonesia, including the road between Pangkalpinang and Payung, Tobaoli, and Mentok; and the Mangong Forest Reserve near Petingdang between Desa Kurau and Desa Balilik. It occurs in habitats from swamps and forest streams to hill streams, usually in black water. This 4-inch fish is light gray-brown with a greenish throat, and three horizontal black lines along the flank, the central line most prominent. Its most striking characters are the slightly elongated anal and dorsal fins of the male, and a pointed snout with a dark band from the snout to the end of the gill cover.

Betta ideii.

The narrow head resembles that of bubble-nesters, although this fish is a known mouth-brooder.

Unimaculata Group

The *Betta unimaculata* species group includes *B. unimaculata*, *B. gladiator*, *B. pallifina*, *B. compuncta*, and *B. ideii*.

Betta ideii TAN AND NG, 2006 is restricted to coastal streams of far southeastern Borneo. It has a distinctive orange patch from the upper jaw to the eye (similar to *B. patoti* with which it has been confused), a black chin bar, iridescent light blue gill cover, and a dark body as an adult. Males are larger than females and black, and smaller females are dark brown with up to nine vertical dark bars.

Betta pallifina TAN AND NG, 2005 occurs in clear upland, neutral tributaries of the Barito River in Kalimantan (southern Borneo). This member of the *B. unimaculata* species group

Betta pallifina *from Muara Taweh, Sumatra, prespawning.*

Betta pallifina.

has been frequently illustrated, with colors that run the gamut from orange tan to brilliant blue on the gill covers and fins. None of these images show the diagnostic lanceolate caudal fin of *B. pallifina* that appears in the original description, and modern photographs may represent other species gathered by commercial collectors. Otherwise the male (of whatever species are in the hobby) incubates the eggs until the release of the fry about two weeks later.

Betta unimaculata POPTA, 1905 averages less than 6 inches, males are larger than females, and sexual characters develop when half grown (more intense blue-green iridescence and larger size in males, horizontal stripes in females). Known from many localities in Borneo (Barito, Pulau Laut, Mahakam, Labuk, and Sabah) in streams, rivers, ditches, trickles, and puddles, in moderately hard, neutral (pH 7.5) water, hidden among vegetation. If the tank is well vegetated (to protect the female in case she is not ready for spawning), spawning should occur around evening or even at night. As with several mouthbrooders, the female may remain near the brooding male and even fend off other fishes. Easily bred, the male incubates the 50–80 eggs for a week and a half, after which the half-inch (7 mm) fry take live *Artemia* nauplii at once and grow rapidly even while in the parental tank, reaching half their adult size in six months. Maturity takes a year.

Betta compuncta TAN AND NG, 2006 of the *Betta unimaculata* species group occurs in headwaters of the Mahakam River in central Borneo

Betta cf. unimaculata *new var. from Malek.*

Betta compuncta.

where the river originates from a higher eleva-
tion swamp. The lower half may have a broad,
dark horizontal stripe. The male is orange-brown
with a black chin bar, blue gill cover, blue iridescent scales elsewhere, and a yellow band in the
anal fin. The female is marked to the rear with
black-spotted scales forming a network of spots
about five scales deep, less deeply colored and
has an orange band in the anal fin.

Betta gladiator TAN AND NG, 2005 is a large,
aggressive member of the Betta unimaculata

species group of mouthbrooders. It was found in
an upland blackwater stream in the Malian River
basin in Sabah, Borneo. The IBC recommended
a covered tank not less than 55 gallons for a
breeding pair, with caves and plants to protect
the female. The water should be cool and acidic
(less than pH 6.0). The male incubates the eggs
and the fry are released after two weeks.

Picta Group

The Betta picta species group (B. picta, B.
taeniata, B. pallida, B. falx, B. simplex) share
prominent dark margins in the anal and caudal
fins, an iridescent gill cover, and small size.
They also have 21–26 anal fin rays, eight–10
dorsal fin rays, 27–29 vertebrae, 27–30 lateral
scales and five–six subdorsal scales.

Betta picta CUVIER AND VALENCIENNES, 1846 was
recently redescribed by Tan and Kottelat (1998)
in an effort to correctly identify this fish, whose
type specimens are no longer available. Body
colors vary from light with a dark back and two

Betta falx.

or three dark horizontal lines, the middle one ending in a dark basicaudal spot, to purple with bands or blotches. The anal fin may have rows of purple spots or, more often, is purple from the base to the middle or more of the fin, where the fin then becomes adorned with a broad blue submarginal band, extending almost to the margin of the fin where it is replaced by a black and then light edge. It differs from *B. simplex, B. falx,* and *B. taeniata* in having yellow-gold rather than greenish-blue opercle scales, a narrow rather than wide distal band in the anal and caudal fins, in scale and fin ray counts, and in the relative locations of the fins to one another.

Betta picta is a hill stream fish, not occurring in lowlands. Peaceful, it may be kept in groups in cool (75°F/24°C) water. Mass spawning is triggered by a water change. This curious behavior may be an adaptation to unpredictable heavy rains that suddenly increase stream flow. Following mass spawning with similar incubation periods, a large group of fry from many broods would be released simultaneously in a nursery area where their numbers would reduce the likelihood of predation on any individual. Analogous phenomena would be synchronous coral spawning, herd behavior in African savannah herbivores, and schooling in forage fish, all providing safety in numbers. A further benefit of synchronous and periodic spawning is that it will not support a predator population requiring a continuous food supply.

The abundant *Betta picta* fry (from many males) are easy to raise on *Artemia* nauplii alone, reaching adult size in half a year. It has sometimes been reported as "*B. trifasciata,*" a synonym. It differs from other members of the group in having a reddish rather than blue distal band in the anal and caudal fins

Betta taeniata.

of the males. The male also has distinct bars across the back (faint in *B. picta* and absent in the other species). The fish was reported as *B. picta* by Weber and De Beaufort in 1912 and Bleeker in 1879, in part, and also by Kottelat and coworkers (in part) as recently as 1993. Witte and Schmidt's (1992) *B. "edithae"* from the Jambi area was probably this species. *Betta picta* is a frequent and easy spawner that will fill all available tank space with offspring. It is not particularly attractive, and you will likely have difficulty disposing of production. Like an alley cat, this is the gift that keeps on giving.

Betta taeniata REGAN, 1910 from Borneo and Sarawak is a lined mouthbrooder attaining much larger size than *B. picta.* Otherwise it is much like *B. picta* in its variation from solid to three-lined on a dull clay to yellowish body, with a dark band in the anal and caudal fins submargined in a lighter band. Its most striking coloration is the green iridescent markings on its gill covers. It prefers cool (75°F/24°C) water but, as expected from its great range, tolerates a variety of water conditions and temperatures. It is easily bred, but

is not especially attractive and has never become popular. In some literature it has been reported as *B. trifasciata* or *B. macrophthalma*.

Betta simplex KOTTELAT, 1994 from Krabi province in Thailand is a robust member of its group with an unusually large head. The

Betta taeniata.

body is light reddish brown (male) or yellowish brown (female) with black horizontal lines confined to the head at the jaws, eye, and gill cover (male) or extending the entire length of the flank (female). The unpaired fins are margined in a thin white line, submargined in a broad blue-black band particularly prominent in the anal fin, and a lighter band still further inward. The throat and gill cover are iridescent green (male) or white (female). The habitat was the shoreline of a deep (thirty feet) pool in a hilly limestone (karst) area, with cool, medium hard water of pH 7.0.

Betta pallida SCHINDLER AND SCHMIDT, 2004 from Narathiwit province in southern Thailand has a lanceolate caudal fin and three distinctive, dark horizontal stripes. It differs from

Betta simplex.

other species in its group by lacking a wide dark band on the anal and lower caudal fins, and in having a chin bar. Water conditions at the original habitat site were pH 6.3–6.5, 69–82 microsiemens per centimeter conductivity, and 79°F/26°C at depths of 20–50 cm.

Betta falx TAN AND KOTTELAT, 1998 resembles *B. picta*, but is a lowland, swamp forest fish, not occurring in hill streams. It occurs in swamp forests around Langkat in Jambi province, and in Deli (now Medan) in north Sumatra. In the Batang Hari basin in Jambi province it was found among submerged bank vegetation in quiet waters of low to neutral pH (4.7–6.8) associated with *Betta* sp. aff. *fusca*, *Parosphromenus sumatranus*, *Sphaerichthys osphromenoides*, *Trichogaster trichopterus*, *T. leeri*, *Trichopsis vittata*, and *Belontia hasseltii*. In aquaria it spawns about every two weeks, the male brooding the eggs.

Pugnax Group

The *Betta pugnax* species group (*B. pugnax*, *B. pulchra*, *B. breviobesus*, *B. stigmosa*, *B. raja*, *B. lehi*, *B. apollon*, *B. ferox*, *B. cracens*, *B. kuehnei*, *B. prima*, *B. enisae*, perhaps others) consists of upland species from flowing waters in Borneo, Sumatra, Vietnam, Cambodia, and Thailand. They all have a large head, 28 to 40 percent of the body length from the tip of the snout to the base of the tail fin, the body is brown with greenish to bluish scales on the gill covers and often the body, throat, and belly, and a lance-shaped, elongate caudal fin (round in *B. kuehnei*) that, in the males of some species, has concentric dark rings.

Betta pugnax *male.*

Betta pulchra.

Betta pugnax CANTOR, 1849 was redescribed by Tan and Tan (1996) from the Malay peninsula. Populations occur on Penang immediately offshore from the Malaysian province of Kedah, in the provinces of Terenggann, Pahang, Perak, Selangor, Johor in the south, and on Singapore. *Betta pugnax* is slender with a robust head whose length would fit 2.5–3.6 times within the standard length of the fish (from the tip of the snout to the base of the tail fin). It is usually brown with bluish-green iridescent scales on the gill covers extending to the chest and belly. Juveniles and females have

two horizontal lines along the body ending in a common basicaudal spot, and two stripes on the side of the head. Adults have elongate and broadly lance-shaped caudal fins. Males have indistinct dark concentric bars in the caudal fin, but otherwise the sexes are similar.

The natural habitats are usually clear, sluggish to rapidly flowing, unstained, cool, neutral to slightly alkaline pH (7.1–7.5), upland streams with sandy or rubble bottoms, along quiet, densely vegetated banks and coves, over vegetation and leaf litter. This peaceful fish readily spawns in large, well planted tanks with high quality, cool (70°–75°F/21–24°C) water. I've had several but unwitnessed spawns, and one witnessed unsuccessful spawn in which the female ate the eggs. The large, guppy-size fry take *Artemia* nauplii at once upon release less than two weeks later, and were half grown in six months.

Betta cracens TAN AND NG, 2005 was collected from a swamp forest floor on Sumatra. This member of the *Betta pugnax* species group of

Betta cracens.

mouthbrooders has the unpaired fins of the male elongated in addition to a lanceolate caudal fin. It is gray to tan with blue margin on the anal fin and a short black stripe from the snout to the edge of the gill cover. It prefers cool water. The male incubates the eggs and fry for about two weeks.

Betta lehi TAN AND NG, 2005 is placed in the *Betta pugnax* species group of mouthbrooders. Native to both sides of the lower Kapuas River basin in western Borneo at the Malaysian and Indonesian border, *Betta lehi* lives in small, darkly stained streams and backwaters having sufficient flow to scour the bottom free of silt and is most common along quiet, vegetated shorelines. The bottom here is often littered with leaves, twigs, and branches, and the overhead tree canopy shades and cools the water. The pH is neutral. The male incubates the eggs and fry up to two weeks, and fry take *Artemia* nauplii upon release.

Betta raja TAN AND NG, 2005 may be a complex of species occurring in different rivers on Sumatra. The locality of each stock should be labeled, and individuals from different rivers not mixed. This member of the *Betta pugnax* species group lives in shaded lowland swamps, in cool, clear, or stained water. A standard setup would be a covered 20-gallon bare tank with dried hardwood leaves, twigs, and branches, plastic (PVC, ABS) tubes, or overturned flower pots for spawning sites, low-light vegetation such as *Cryptocoryne* or *Najas*, and a diet of live and frozen foods. The male incubates the eggs and fry for two weeks, and the fry take *Artemia* nauplii as a first food.

Betta stigmosa TAN AND NG, 2005 is a small (two-inch) member of the *Betta pugnax* species group of mouthbrooders that occurs in

Betta lehi *habitat.*

clear, highland streams of the Sekayu Recreation Forest on the east side of the Malay Peninsula above the falls, but may be more widespread. The male incubates the brood for one or two weeks. The fish is not demanding, and a 15-gallon tank is sufficient for breeding.

Betta kuehnei SCHINDLER AND SCHMIDT, 2008 is the only species of this group with a rounded caudal fin, a single dark stripe on the gill cover behind the eye, and no dark chin bar. The male is iridescent blue-green, and horizontal body stripes appear only when it is stressed. The iris is red and the anal fin blue-green in its outer third to half. Males incubate 40 to 80 eggs for about 12 days, and the fry at a half inch (7 mm) take *Artemia* nauplii as a first food.

Betta pulchra TAN AND TAN, 1996 differs from *B. pugnax* in having a narrowly lance-shaped caudal fin, a more robust body, greater distribution of greenish-blue rather than bluish-green iridescent scales extending over the flanks, dark concentric or ladderlike marks on

the dorsal fin but not the caudal, and red and black margins on the anal fin. Even the edges of the pelvic (ventral) fins are iridescent green. *B. pulchra* is found only in blackwater habitats in Pontian, in the southern province of Johor, on the southwestern side of the Malaysian peninsula quite close to Singapore. It was suspected of being a blackwater phenotypic variant of *B. pugnax*, but the two species were found to breed true no matter the water quality in which they were raised. Associates of *B. pulchra* include *Belontia hasselti*, *Sphaerichthys osphromenoides*, *Parosphro-*

Betta kuehnei, *Batang Merbau/Kelantan/Malaysia.*

Collecting **Betta lehi.**

menus sp., *Trichopsis vittata*, *Betta bellica*, and *B. imbellis*. It is never found with *B. pugnax*, which does not occur in this type of habitat.

   Betta breviobesus TAN AND KOTTELAT, 1998 was described from the Kapuas River basin (mostly the upper basin) in Kalimantan Barat, Indonesia, on the island of Borneo. It occurs in small forest streams of neutral to slightly acidic pH (6–7). It has been caught in traps used to collect baitfish. Otherwise there is little information on its habitat. It lacks a dark chin bar (found in *B. pugnax*, *B. pulchra*, and *B. prima*), and has dark margins on the caudal and anal

Betta ferox.

fins (lacking in *B. pugnax*, *B. fusca*, *B. pulchra*, *B. prima*, and *B. schalleri*).

   Betta prima KOTTELAT, 1994 is known from Chantaburi and Trat provinces in southeastern Thailand and from the Phnom Penh to Sihanoukville road in Cambodia. It was found in small creeks and swamps, but no other habitat information was provided. It is distinguished from other members of its group by its small size (less than 2 inches without the tail fin), a complete (uninterrupted) lower head stripe that continues onto the gill cover, the caudal fin without central ray extensions, and the dorsal fin rays not extended. It is light brown, darker above, with three dark horizontal stripes along the flank. The throat and gill cover are slightly iridescent green. Rows of brown spots decorate the dorsal fin, the caudal fin is colorless, and the anal fin has a narrow dark margin. It resembles a member of the *B. picta* group in size and the margin on the anal fin, but has more rays in the anal fin and no dark margin in the caudal fin.

   Betta ferox SCHINDLER AND SCHMIDT, 2006 is known only from Bori Pat, near Hat Yai at the narrowest portion of southern Thailand. This large, reddish brown fish lives among roots and vegetation in an upland, fast-flowing, clear river with a sand and gravel bed. The throat and gill cover may be iridescent blue-green, and its incomplete chin bar is not as distinctive as in the related *B. apollon*.

   Betta apollon SCHINDLER AND SCHMIDT, 2006 occurs only in Thailand's forested hill streams. It inhabits soft, slightly acidic water among plants, leaf litter, and roots close to shore, but extends to deeper, swifter water among boulders. The last ray at the top of the gill arch is elongated, white, and flattened in older males. This is the only member of its group with a chin bar.

Betta apollon.

Betta tomi.

Betta enisae KOTTELAT, 1995, a member of this group from Borneo, has a dark gray-brown body, pointed caudal fin, iridescent green scales on the gill covers and black-edged caudal and anal fins, each with a prominent, broad, bright blue submargin that is characteristic of the species.

Waseri Group

The Betta waseri group (B. waseri, B. pardalotos, B. tomi, B. spilotogena, B. pi, B. renata, B. hipposideros, B. chloropharynx) is characterized by color zonation of the eyes, and diagnostic throat and lower jaw patterns. Many are large fish (2½ inch/6.4 cm body length, exclusive of the tail fin) with yellow-brown bodies and iridescent gold belly and gill cover scales. The most striking character is the eye, the black pupil surrounded by an iridescent golden iris with a thin red line in the middle of the golden zone all around the eye. The group is restricted to the peninsula of Malaysia, southern Thailand, Sumatra, Pulau Banka, and the Riau Archipelago. None is as yet known from Borneo.

Betta waseri KRUMMENACHER, 1986 was described from a single specimen collected from Pahang in peninsular Malaysia, and has the pattern characteristic of the group, including a pair of teardrop shaped black marks on the chin.

Betta tomi NG AND KOTTELAT, 1994 from Johore (peninsular Malaysia) has more regular spotting below a doubled black flank band, quite dark jaws and chin markings, and the male is reddish brown with a lighter chest.

Betta renata TAN, 1998 was collected from Rantau Panjang and Pematang Lumut, in Jambi

Betta renata *from Jambi.*

Betta pi.

swamp water of low pH (4.1) in a logged area. In the same waters occur *Rasbora kalochroma*, *Betta coccina*, *B. simorum*, *Sphaerichthys osphromenoides*, *Nandus nebulosus*, *Belontia hasselti*, *Puntius hexazona*, *Mystus bimaculatus*, *Clarias teijsmanni*, *Kottelatlimia pristes* (a cobitid), and other fishes.

Betta pi TAN, 1998, the northernmost member of the *B. waseri* group, was collected in a cleared peat swamp forest at Mae Nam Tod Deng near Sungai Kolok, Narathiwat province, in southern Thailand. The water was soft, pH 6.0, and up to 4 feet deep over a soft bottom. The only other fishes were *Channa lucius* and *Parosphromenus* cf. *paludicola*. The black pigment on the lower jaw is contiguous with two vertical black lines that bend outward at the bottom, providing the illusion of a Greek letter *pi*. The gill cover has black markings and a black lower edge, but no iridescent green. The anal fin has a dark blue edge.

Betta spilotogena NG AND KOTTELAT, 1994 is known from Pulau Bintan, in the Riau Archipelago of Indonesia.

Betta pardalotos TAN, 2009, also from Pulau Bintan, has heavily spotted gill covers with two rows of spots extending to the throat and other spots beyond the gills. The dark bar on both jaws surrounds an unmarked or unpigmented center. It occurs with other anabantoid species in freshwater streams.

Betta hipposideros NG AND KOTTELAT, 1994 is known from Selangor on the Malay Peninsula and has the black markings on the chin that define the group.

province, around Lahat (Sumatra Selatan), and in the Indragiri basin (Riau), all in Sumatra, Indonesia. This is the fish that Weber and De Beaufort incorrectly identified as *B. anabatoides* in 1922. Its kidney-shaped black throat marking is not connected to the black lower jaw. There is no margin on the anal fin, but there is a margin on the lower edge of the gill cover. It was found in darkly stained peat forest

Betta hipposideros.

Betta antoni *from Tanyan.*

Female **Betta antoni.**

Betta chloropharynx KOTTELAT AND NG, 1994 was collected in leaf litter from a shallow pool in a clear, black creek in a second growth forest south of Pangkalpinang on the road to Toboali south of Koba, Banka, Indonesia. It has large chin markings of black circles surrounding iridescent green inclusions. The caudal fin is rhomboid to slightly lanceolate. The body is yellow-brown, darker above, with an iridescent golden spot on the gill cover, and broad light band on the flank that seems to emphasize darker surrounding bands above and below. Spotting appears reduced on the lower flank.

Betta antoni TAN AND NG, is native to the lower Kapuas River basin of Borneo. It occurs in small creeks near Sauggau and Narya Pinoh. It is the slimmest member of the *Betta akarensis* group, with iridescent blue scales on the flank, a black lower lip and black chin bar, and iridescence on the reddish-brown anal fin. The caudal fin is rounded but may have protruding central rays, and is always edged in white. Depending on mood, the body may have several vertical

Betta waseri *blackwater ditch.*

dark bands and indistinct markings on the head, or it may have two distinct horizontal dark lines along the entire flank from the nape to the eye to the top and middle of the caudal peduncle, combined with dark bars radiating from the eye.

Betta obscura TAN AND NG. 2005 was reported from the Lahei River, a tributary of the Barito River, in the southern portion (Kalimantan) of Borneo. It is a cool water fish, suggesting a montane origin. It's a small mouthbrooder, with the male incubating the eggs. Provide a 10-gallon, densely vegetated tank with a tight cover and abundant hiding places.

Akarensis Group

The *Betta akarensis* species group (*B. akarensis, B. balunga, B. chini, B. pinguis, B. aurigens, B. antoni, B. ibanorum, B. obscura*, and perhaps unnamed species) is restricted to Borneo. Members of the group have a black stripe on the cheek from the tip of the snout to the eye, another complete lower stripe, and a post-orbital stripe from behind the eye to the gill opening. There are no iridescent scales on the gill covers. The caudal fin is rhomboidal rather than rounded, and has concentric dark markings in the membranes.

Betta akarensis REGAN, 1910 was described from a single juvenile specimen from Sungai Akar in central Sarawak. This is the same fish named *Betta climacura* by VIERKE in 1984 from Rampayoh in northern Sarawak. *B. akarensis* varies from solid dark gray to lighter with three bold black lines, the middle one passing through the eye to the lips, these lines separated by horizontal rows of black spots. Each pair of black lines with its included black spots may darken to form a dark band. Males have elongated unpaired fins, but no striking colors.

Betta aurigens TAN AND LIM, 2004 occurs on Great Natuna Island, which has geographic and biological affinities (they were once connected) with Borneo. It has a complete chin bar, a black stripe from the snout to the eye, and another from the eye to the edge of the gill cover. It lives in densely vegetated black water pools in an inland forest among a variety of other fishes. Males have gold scales on the flanks and belly, but not on the gill cover. The dorsal and caudal fins are marked by at least 20 black bars, and the anal fin is edged in black.

Betta balunga HERRE, 1940 from the Balung River near Tawau in eastern Sabah of northern Borneo is a robust mouthbrooder with a dark

Betta akarensis.

Betta chini.

wise is not remarkable. The fish was collected from Sungai Letang, near Kampung Kandung Suli (Kecamatan Jongkong) in the middle Kapuas River basin, Kalimantan Barat, on the island of Borneo. The specimens were obtained by fishermen who caught them in a small blackish water stream on hook and line among large numbers of *Betta enisae* and smaller numbers of *B. dimidiata*, to be used as bait for a notopterid.

gray body and blue highlights in the anal and sometimes lower caudal fin. A broad black line from the lips through the eye across the gill plates continues to a basicaudal spot on the caudal peduncle, but the band may disappear to the rear of the gill covers.

Betta chini NG, 1993 was described from logged peat swamps along a road between Beaufort and Kota Kinabalu in east Sabah, East Malaysia, on the island of Borneo, associated with *Rasbora eithovenii, Luciocephalus pulcher*, and a catfish (*Ompok*). It has dark scales with light edges, a black line through the lips, eyes, and gill cover, a broad black mark under the chin, and a strikingly bold black band behind the eye and extending to the lower base of the tail fin; above this band is a narrower but equally conspicuous black band extending from behind the gill cover to the upper base of the tail. The anal fin is brown with dark edging in the female, and elongate in the male, and both sexes have delicately spotted unpaired fins.

Betta pinguis TAN AND KOTTELAT, 1998 is the most deep-bodied member of this species group, with the most densely pigmented gill cover. It differs from other members of its group in scales and fin ray counts, but other-

Foerschi Group

The *Betta foerschi* species group contains at least four beautiful species (*B. foerschi, B. strohi, B. rubra,* and *B. mandor*), characterized by a dark body and two orange bars on the gill covers of the male. They are swamp inhabitants and do best in soft, acidic, tea-colored water.

Betta foerschi VIERKE, 1979 occurs in the Kahajan and Sampit River drainages in Borneo. The male is reddish-brown above, bluish-black below, with the colors extending into the unpaired fins. Each gill cover has two vertical yellow-orange bars separated by a black bar,

Betta foerschi.

and the iris is iridescent. The female is reddish-brown with seven indistinct black bars extending from the base of the anal fin into the lower two thirds of the flank and more black on the caudal fin. Linke (1989) described aquarium spawning in which the male picked up the eggs directly or the female picked them up and passed them to the male. Two spawns resulted in 38 and 46 fry that reached 7.9–9.1 in/20–23 mm three weeks later. Gilbert Limhengco fed live food and had them spawn at a half flowerpot cave following a water change.

Even prettier is *Betta strohi* SCHALLER AND KOTTELAT, 1989 from the Jelai or Bila River basin in Borneo. The male is iridescent green to midnight blue-black, with a pointed caudal fin, black edged unpaired fins, and gill covers ornately painted with brilliant yellow bars.

Betta mandor TAN AND NG, 2006 is known from Anjungan and Mandor in the lower Kapuas River basin of Borneo. The male is black, the female brown, and twin red bars on the male's gill cover are distinctive. The head is marked with yellow-brown spots, and a portion of the iris of the eye is often bright green. The

unpaired fins are dark, sometimes iridescent, with white margins. In earlier aquarium books, the fish was labeled "Betta from Mandor."

Betta rubra PERUGIA, 1893 was rediscovered in the (now peaceful) Aceh province at the western tip of Sumatra and is available. Both sexes of this small member of the *Betta foerschi* group of male mouthbrooders are generally light-bodied with a dark horizontal band through the middle of the flank. The male has twin red cheek bars, but during spawning his throat can become vivid red, orange, gold, or blue, depending on the angle of the light. This is the only mouthbrooder with a splash of red pigment on the mid-flank of many, but not all, females. The male has extensive red patches or bars that occupy most of the flank. Unpaired fins in both sexes during spawning are pale iridescent green in the center, wine red to black toward the outside, and edged in a blueish-white line. During display the rear portion of the iris of the eye becomes deep blue-green in both sexes. Outside spawning, the fish is generally light with a dark stripe, similar to other mouthbrooders, but red blotches are nearly always visible and diagnostic on males.

Pete Liptrot and Paul Dixon of the Bolton Aquarium near Manchester, UK, reported that care is generally simple—they are tolerant of local water chemistry, accept most foods, and continue to be robust after more than four years. The most vivid coloration is seen only briefly during spawning or aggressive displays, when males frequently "flash" at one another. Otherwise, they fade to ordinary. Dixon distributed many offspring to the hobby in Europe. The brooding male is usually moved to

Betta mandor *male from Mandor, Borneo.*

a nursery tank to maximize survival of young. The 30–40 eggs require two weeks to develop before release. If left with the parents, some will survive. *Piscinoodinium* (velvet disease) can be a problem with these fish. Flubendazole sprinkled on the surface is prophylactic. *Betta rubra* lives in clear or turbid, slow-moving to stagnant, forested black water pools and streams. The bottoms are littered with dead leaves, branches, and tree roots. It also occurs in thick shoreline vegetation of those same waters. It has misleadingly been called the Toba Betta, but that name should be discarded. Lake Toba is a volcanic lake high in the midst of Sumatra's central mountain chain, and *B. rubra* is a lowland fish from the western coastal plain.

Betta ibanorum TAN AND NG, 2005 of the *Betta akarensis* species group is widely distributed in Sarawak, the Malaysian territory located in northern Borneo. Its vast geographic and ecological range east and west, coastal and mountainous, is compounded by its variation in color from tan to gold-brown with indistinct darker horizontal stripes or vertical bands. At present these populations are all considered the same species, but the critical aquarist will know the origin of his population and not mix or breed stocks from other localities. How *B. ibanorum* came to occupy habitats as different as clear mountain rivers and an acidic coastal black water swamp could be explained as either a fish of enormous tolerance and early dispersal, or perhaps human intervention. It's a large fish, more than 4 inches total length, and exploited locally as food. Humans who exploit specific foods often disperse them. Otherwise consider it a jumper requiring a large, covered aquarium with abundant hiding places. Maintain a high (80°F/26.6°C) temperature,

Betta ibanorum.

and feed only live and frozen foods. The male incubates the eggs and fry for two to three weeks and should be moved to the grow-out tank (not less than 20 gallons) until the fry are all released.

Albimarginata Group

Equally beautiful mouthbrooders are in the *Betta albimarginata* group, consisting of *B. albimarginata* and *B. channoides* from Borneo. These species have wide, flat heads and a dorsal fin insertion only slightly behind the insertion of the first anal fin rays. They differ from all other *Betta* species in having more spines in the anal fin (9 to 12 *vs.* zero to four) and fewer soft (articulated) rays (11 to 13 *vs.* 18 to 32). Like members of the previous group, they are swamp dwellers and do best in soft, acid, tea-stained water.

B. albimarginata KOTTELAT AND NG, 1994 occurs in Borneo's Sebuku River drainage of Kalimantan Timur. It occupies the leaf litter and vegetation in shallows near the shore of forest streams with moderate current. The flanks are yellowish-brown to reddish-brown, and the back and top of the head are yellow to

Male **Betta albimarginata.**

Female **Betta albimarginata.**

white with black spots. All fins except the clear pectorals have a broad white margin and a black submargin, with red in the remaining fin area, another unique character of this species. A peaceful fish, pairs do well in moderately lit, well-vegetated, moderately soft (140 ppm hardness), neutral (pH 7.0–7.2), peat moss-stained water in 5- to 10-gallon tanks. Feed live *Daphnia*, baby brine shrimp, blackworms and/or tubifex worms, supplemented with frozen brine shrimp and bloodworms. Keep snails

or tadpoles in the tank as scavengers, and keep these tanks covered. Provide driftwood or a flowerpot as a spawning cave.

B. channoides KOTTELAT AND NG, 1994 was collected in leaf litter and among plant roots from the Sungei Behernas, a swiftly flowing blackwater tributary of the middle Mahakam River near Mujab and Muarapahu in Kalimantan Timur on the island of Borneo. It differs from *B. albimarginata* by one more anal spine (12), one or two more anal rays (23 to 25), and smaller and more numerous scales. Only preserved juvenile specimens are known, but they have a pale and probably yellowish-white top of the head and back, and spotting on the fins. There are sufficient marking and morphological differences to separate the two closely related species.

A third member of the group is found at Malinau in the Sesajap River basin in northern Borneo. It has wider white margins on its unpaired fins. Yet a fourth population has been collected in the lower Mahakam River basin around Panpang, in central Borneo.

Betta channoides.

Betta patoti.

Patoti Group

The *Betta patoti* species group (*B. patoti* and two to four unnamed species) occurs in Borneo. Adults have pointed fins, and the caudal of the male may be spade shaped. The body may be unremarkable, spotted, or covered with iridescent scales. Like most mouthbrooders, they do best in clear, cool, neutral, well-oxygenated water.

Betta patoti WEBER AND DE BEAUFORT, 1922 is slender with a large head and large eyes, and is distinct in having 11 dark bars on the body. The photograph in Schäfer's Aqualog said to be from Timur in Borneo is a misidentification of *B. unimaculata*.

An unnamed species in the *B. patoti* species group from the same location was blue-black, with iridescent highlights at the pectoral insertion and the rear of the gill cover, and white edging on the dorsal fin and tips of the pelvics. Otherwise the unpaired fins are marked with a dark network pattern.

Another unnamed member of this complex was collected by Linke from Laut Island off the southeast coast of Borneo. It occurs in fast flowing rocky mountain streams of medium hardness and neutral pH, and in industrial bays. This 5-inch long fish is reddish with heavily spotted fins, a slightly spade-shaped caudal fin, and abundant iridescent green scales on the chin and gill covers, but not extending above the level of the eye.

Betta patoti.

Water Quality

Water quality for almost all the mouthbrooding bettas can be satisfied with dechlorinated tap water and no heater (most come from cool upland streams). Tap water is generally neutral to alkaline and moderately hard to hard depending on the limestone content of the water supply aquifer or basin.

These conditions are similar to conditions in many upland streams. Some mouthbrooders are stimulated to spawn by a massive (50-75 percent) water change.

Tank Size

As a rule, mouthbrooders attain greater adult size than bubblenesters and require larger quarters. Breeding tanks for small mouthbrooders (B. picta, B. edithae) should be at least 10 gallons, and for the larger mouthbrooders (B. pugnax) at least 20 gallons.

To Jar or Not to Jar

Mouthbrooders should not be housed in individual jars. Mouthbrooders, in general, are more gill dependent

Spawning Conditions for Mouthbrooders

TOP VIEW

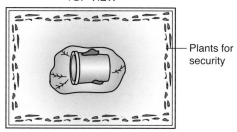

Plants for security

SIDE VIEW

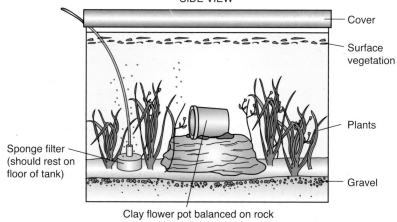

Cover

Surface vegetation

Plants

Sponge filter (should rest on floor of tank)

Gravel

Clay flower pot balanced on rock

and less labyrinth dependent than swamp-inhabiting bubblenesters. These stream fishes are accustomed to the high oxygen concentrations of running water (or in a tank, aerated or filtered water). In individual jars, water stagnates and oxygen levels become depressed. The low oxygen concentration also depresses pH, stresses the fish, and increases the risk of disease.

Caves

Some mouthbrooders spawn in the open and others prefer an enclosed area such as the shade of a log, branch, or rock. Some *(B. edithae)* prefer a cave. A cave or cavern can be supplied by a large diameter segment of PVC plumbing pipe (available at a hardware store) or a flowerpot laid on its side. Flowerpots should have the drain holes widened or broken out entirely to prevent bettas from being trapped in the narrow opening.

Vegetation

Java moss or other live plants should be included in stock, breeding, and grow-out tanks. Plants remove nitrates (growth inhibitors), toxic metals, and other pollutants, regenerating water quality. They also provide protection for fry and refuges for battered individuals.

Lighting

Breeding tanks should be dimly illuminated. Exposure to temporary sunlight is beneficial, but the tank should be shaded most of the day. Mouthbrooders kept under 24-hour lighting are less likely to spawn than those exposed to an 8:16 to 12:12 light cycle. Although the growth of fry is increased under 24-hour continuous lighting, water changes are far more effective growth enhancers.

Should the Brooding Parent Be Moved?

Upland stream mouthbrooders may community spawn in response to a water change, resulting in several males brooding simultaneously in the same large tank. These males should be removed to individual 10-gallon aquariums for brooding and release of fry. Because it takes 24 hours for freshly spawned fertilized eggs to "harden" or withstand mechanical stress, it's a good idea to wait until late the next day to move these males.

The brooding male of mouthbrooders housed in pairs and accustomed to soft, acidic swamp water should not be moved. Rather, the female should be removed and transferred to another aquarium two or three days after spawning. Be certain that water quality in the new aquarium is similar to that of the breeding aquarium.

Feeding

Do not place frozen, freeze-dried, or dried foods in any aquarium containing a brooding male. The male does not eat during the incubation period. The fry will require food shortly after release, but there is often enough natural food (copepods, ostracods, etc.) in the tank to provide immediate needs. As soon as fry are seen in the aquarium, begin light feedings of live baby brine shrimp. I always keep live *Daphnia* in all my acidic water mouthbrooder tanks as a regenerating food supply for the adults and an immediate food supply for offspring.

TANKS FOR SIAMESE FIGHTING FISH

Siamese fighting fish thrive in community tanks of small fishes, but are weak swimmers, so do not place them with cichlids, catfishes (other than suckermouth catfishes), barbs, African tetras, or larger predators.

Generally, livebearers, danios, South American tetras, and gouramies are safe cohabitants of the community tank. Keep only one male in the tank, but you can keep several females. The tank should not have strong currents from power-heads or canister filters. You can induce male displays by attaching a mirror to the side glass.

Dedicated Tanks

Many breeders house male and female show fish in individual jars. Fish not of show quality may be grouped in tanks, the males removed if they become belligerent. In bigger tanks (55 gallons), males of a single spawn raised together (a cohort) may not become belligerent until half grown, while those raised in smaller tanks become aggressive earlier.

You can keep males in quart or gallon jars or flat-sided drum bowls. Glass jars can be cleaned in an automatic dishwasher, whereas

Betta pallifina *juveniles from Muara Taweh.*

plastic becomes opaque with heat. Mason jars, available from your supermarket, are widely used by breeders. Gallon jars are available from fast-food restaurants, often at no charge, but you will get more cooperation by offering a dollar per jar.

Selecting Fishes

Fancy strains of Siamese fighting fish are available in veiltail, double-tail, blue, red, green, black, yellow, cambodia, butterfly, half-moon, koi, and marble. Breeding a red with a red will produce 50 to 100 percent red off-spring, as we will see later, but breeding a red with a blue may result in 100 percent muddy offspring. Get males and females of the same strain if that is the type you want to raise; even then, it is unlikely that all their offspring will resemble the parents.

Bettas in stores may be housed in jars, in divided betta tanks (barracks), in perforated plastic containers hung inside an ordinary aquarium, or in individual plastic bins mounted

━━━━ T I P ━━━━

Carding Male Bettas

Keep an opaque sheet of paper, cardboard, or plastic between jars of male bettas. When the card is removed, the males will display at one another, fins spread and gill covers flaring. If the cards are not replaced, the males become used to each other and stop displaying.

on a commercial display rack and fitted with an automatic water changer or filter.

If the fish are inactive, rather than swimming easily back and forth or flaring when placed alongside others, they may be poorly cared for and potentially carrying diseases. If the jar needs cleaning or is overgrown with dark slime, especially on the floor, or if the water has an unpleasant odor, buy somewhere else.

Look for cloudy eyes, bruises, bloody patches, or white opaque marks as signs of infection. Fish with drooping fins may not be sick, merely bored because they were not carded in the store. A healthy fish should have clear eyes, unsplit fins, no bite marks, and no white rims or margins on the fins or body. The body should be full but not bloated, and thick; avoid fish that appear sunken and showing their ribs. Discrete fecal droppings should litter the bottom of the jar, indicating regular feeding and normal digestion. Females should be almost obese yet active, with a prominent white egg-spot at the vent (the end of the oviduct), and should swim without struggling to maintain equilibrium.

Catching, bagging, and transferring the fish to a new environment is stressful and increases susceptibility to disease by depressing resistance. Avoiding stress is better than having to treat an avoidable disease.

Water Quality

The many species of *Betta* come from habitats ranging from cool, clear, sandy hill streams to hot, muddy forest floors flooded with black, acidic water. Where a fish is found in nature, however, should not be your guide to its care. Natural habitats are impossible to duplicate in captivity and simultaneously keep clean. No matter where fish come from in the wild, they will do well in clean, neutral pH water devoid of pollutants.

All fish produce ammonia and urea that are converted to nitrites and nitrates by bacteria in the tank. These wastes are growth inhibitors. A crowded tankful of young fighting fish

━━━━ T I P ━━━━

Water Changes

Filtration cannot replace water changes. Filter floss removes particles, activated carbon removes colors and dissolved gases, and ion-exchange resins remove ammonia and other compounds. But they all become saturated and stop working, and none removes growth-inhibiting nitrates. Commercial hatcheries do regular massive water changes to obtain rapid growth and healthy fish.

grows unevenly because faster growing fish put out inhibitors that stunt the slower growers. To grow fish evenly, you could raise them in a large aquarium (55 gallons) with little additional care. If instead you breed them in 10- to 15-gallon tanks, it's necessary to remove the largest individuals to jars and regularly change a portion of the tank water to dilute pollutants.

Temperature Control

The best temperature for *Betta splendens* is 80°F/27°C at which males can breed every two or three days given sufficient females. Females held at 80°F/27°C may spawn every week, those held at 70°F/21°C every three weeks, and those held at 60°F/16°C every four weeks (cited in Gordon, 1955).

Other *Betta* species native to lowland swamps also do better at high temperatures, but hill stream *Betta* species do better at temperatures in the middle to high 70s/24°C. All the species adapt to ambient room temperatures in the middle 70s/24°C.

If you need a heater, keep in mind that they are relatively safe on large tanks and unsafe on small tanks. The safest aquarium heater is your home thermostat, and the riskiest is a commercial aquarium heater. If your house doesn't get cold, then a heater is not necessary except for breeding.

Every heated tank should have an easily read thermometer so tank temperature can be monitored.

TIP

How to Purchase Heaters

The pet industry's heater guideline is 5 watts to the gallon, or a 25-watt heater for a 5-gallon tank. I suggest you cut this in half (a 25-watt heater for a 10-gallon tank). A failed thermostat won't allow the heating element of an undersized heater to cook the tank. Because thermostats eventually fail with age, replace your heater annually with a new unit.

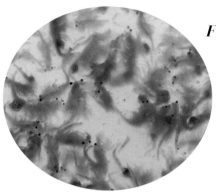

Fish digest foods to use the basic molecules to build the substances they need for structure and function. The few substances they cannot make from precursors must be included in the diet.

Essential substances include vitamins and certain amino acids and fatty acids. Most commercially available foods are deficient in highly unsaturated fatty acids (HUFAs). These are long chain fatty acids in which adjacent carbons share a double bond, as in -C-C=C-C=C- *vs.* the saturated condition, -C-C-C-C-. The number of carbons and the locations of the double bonds distinguish one unsaturated fatty acid from another. Several HUFAs are critical to development in baby fishes.

Major Food Types

In the wild, fighting fish eat ants, mites, mosquito larvae, flies, water fleas, amphipods, isopods, and occasionally small worms or fishes. The insects are the most nutritious of all fish foods because of their high concentrations of proteins, fats, and HUFAs.

In captivity, the most commonly available food insects are mosquito larvae, fruit flies (*Drosophila*), *Daphnia*, glassworms (*Chaoborus*),

A nutritious diet is crucial to good health in **Bettas.**

and bloodworms or midges (chironomids). The crustacean, *Artemia,* is not an insect but almost as nutritious. Other highly nutritious foods are live blackworms, tubifex, microworms, vinegar eels, white worms, and grindal worms.

Artemia (Brine Shrimp)

Betta breeders use *Artemia* as the staple diet, supplemented with live mosquito larvae, frozen bloodworms, meat blends, and flake foods. Baby fish are fed *Artemia* nauplii, with or without smaller foods, and some breeders use nothing but *Artemia* nauplii for bettas of all ages. Brine shrimp are crustaceans of inland saline lakes and coastal salt drying ponds. Adults are harvested as fish food, and the windblown dried cysts are harvested for baby fish food. In the east, brine shrimp are grown in Florida greenhouses. Brine shrimp are mostly parthenogenetic females that produce small brown embryonated cysts in suspended animation. Vacuum-canned cysts remain viable for years. Upon immersion in salt water, the cysts complete development and hatch into nauplii. Cysts sold in pet stores (as "eggs") in plastic packages generally have poor hatch rates. High hatch rates are found with cysts vacuum packed in 15-ounce cans, available through mail-order houses.

Place one-half teaspoon of cysts in a gallon of synthetic sea water with vigorous aeration and strong light. At 24 hours, remove the air, swirl, and strain the slurry through a brine shrimp net (an aquarium net lined with handkerchief cloth). After straining, dump the contents into a jar of cold tap water. After 10 minutes, the nauplii will be at the bottom and the empty cyst shells float at the surface. Pour off the water and shells, leaving the pink/orange mass of nauplii at the bottom, and wipe the remaining shells from the walls with your finger. Resuspend the hatched nauplii by topping the jar off with new tap water, swirl, and feed the nauplii to your fish with a food baster.

Bloodworms (Chironomids)

Bloodworms are larvae of chironomid or sewage flies (midges). The bright red larvae

Freeze-dried bloodworms.

are rich in fats, proteins, and HUFAs. Frozen bloodworms should be thawed in water and dispensed with a food baster. Frozen chunks will choke the fish and freeze their intestines. Bloodworms are harvested from Asian duck ponds and quick frozen for the tropical fish market. Live bloodworms shipped into this country in Kordon breathing bags are available in some pet stores. Some people become allergic to bloodworm proteins. If flu-like symptoms occur when handling this food, discontinue use to avoid severe reactions later.

Daphnia

Daphnia, Ceriodaphnia, Moina, and related cladocerans are called "water fleas." They are not fleas (insects) but crustaceans. Live *Daphnia* from pet stores are seasonal and unreliable. *Daphnia* are easily raised outdoors in sunlight during warm months. Fill a barrel or a wading pool with water and add a handful of dirt. Also place a glass of water plus dirt in full sunlight. Within days, the glass will contain a culture of green algae. Pour that culture into the barrel or pool. When the pool water starts to become green, order your starter culture of *Daphnia* from an aquarium magazine classified advertisement. By the time it arrives, your pool or barrel will have a deep green algal bloom upon which *Daphnia* thrive. When the *Daphnia* become abundant, harvest daily with a coarse net so the smallest individuals can escape to replenish the population. As production drops and the water shifts from green to yellow, do a massive water change to dilute waste products and add more garden soil to replenish algal nutrients. Cold weather depresses production but doesn't kill the culture, which will bloom again in the spring.

You can grow *Daphnia* indoors in 10-gallon or larger tanks. Place intense lighting directly over the tank. Fill with dechlorinated tap water, and aerate with stiff tubing to produce large bubbles. Fine bubbles from an airstone may short circuit your light fixture. Fertilize with dirt or liquid plant food and inoculate with enough green water to barely tint the tank water light green. When the water is opaque green, place your mail order for a *Daphnia* culture. You can feed *Daphnia* with green water or dissolved baker's yeast. Store dry yeast in the refrigerator. Pour a tablespoonful of dry yeast into a gallon of tepid tap water and leave it at room temperature for two days, then store the culture in the refrigerator. Every two days, add a tablespoon of liquid yeast culture to the tank to feed your *Daphnia*. Overfeeding will kill them, whereas underfeeding will only slow their growth. Periodically siphon out most of the water and all the sediment from the bottom, and replace with new tap water. Eventually the culture fails and must be restarted by beginning anew. Never put dried yeast into the *Daphnia* tank as it will kill your culture.

Daphnia.

Blackworms and Red Tubifex

Blackworms and tubifex worms are freshwater aquatic oligochaetes related to earthworms. Both are mixed species of the family Tubificidae. You can purchase portions at some pet stores, and some stores will special order them if you buy two pounds at a time. Red tubifex years ago were collected downstream of sewage treatment plants, and today they are still collected that way in Mexico for shipment here. Keep them in a jar in a sink under slowly running cold tap water. Blackworms are larger

coldwater tubificids from trout farm raceways and the wastewater effluent of vegetable processors. They should be stored in shallow, almost dry dishes in the refrigerator. Every day or two, they should be rinsed with cold, dechlorinated tap water, and the washings discarded. Keep tap water in the refrigerator to maintain a supply of dechlorinated cold water. Both blackworms and red tubifex will live in the gravel in aquariums, but not in jars. Fighting fish sometimes choke to death on live blackworms. For that reason, some people slice them into pieces with a razor blade prior to feeding. Both blackworms and red tubifex worms may carry pathogenic bacteria, and should be purged before feeding to tropical fish. They sometimes

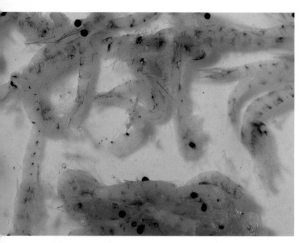

Frozen mysis.

transmit parasitic worms infectious for suckers and catfish, but not fighting fish.

Microworms and Vinegar Eels

Microworms and vinegar eels are minute roundworms (nematodes). Both are excellent

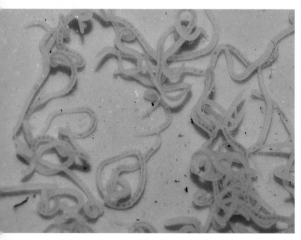

Grindal worms (live).

foods for tiny fry less than a week old. They are not essential, but will increase the number of fry that survive through the early weeks. They can be grown from starter cultures purchased through classified advertisements.

For vinegar eels, buy a quart of malt vinegar, pour half into an empty second jar, and top off both jars with tap water. Cover and pour in the starter culture, and you now have two cultures of vinegar eels. After a few weeks the white cloud at the top of the liquid will be a swarm of vinegar eels. Remove them with a food baster, then strain through a brine shrimp nauplii net, rinse with tap water, and then feed the concentrated worms to the baby fish.

For microworms or walter worms, make a paste of any baby food flakes with water and place it on the bottom of a plastic margarine tub. Sprinkle dried baker's yeast granules and mix into the paste. Place a few drops of starter culture on the paste and cover. A slit in the cover allows gas to escape from the growing yeast. After a few days, the micro-worms swarm over the culture and climb the walls of the tub. Wipe the worms from the walls with your finger, rinse in water to release the worms, and then baste the worms to your baby fish. In two weeks the culture becomes overripe, foul smelling, blackened, liquified, and the worms no longer climb the walls. Begin new cultures and discard the old, using it only as starter material. The new culture does not need yeast, as you will transfer enough with the worms.

White Worms and Grindal Worms

White worms and grindal worms are ter-restrial oligochaetes related to earthworms. Starter cultures are available through classi-

fied advertisements. Both are rich in fats and proteins and excellent conditioning foods for adult fighting fish. Grindal worms are grown at room temperature whereas white worms must be cold. Start a covered wooden or styrofoam box with a 50:50 mix of peat moss and garden soil. Make it damp enough to clump when squeezed, but not wet enough to leak. Mix in the starter culture. Place bread or baby food on the soil. Cover the food with a glass pane, and store. A cold basement is adequate for white worms, but a refrigerator is too cold.

Keep the culture cool and damp as the worms are killed by heat and desiccation. Harvest the worms as they accumulate under the glass pane. Replace bread/flakes as necessary and monitor moisture. Eventually the culture will be contaminated with small black flies. They are annoying but do no harm, and are also food for your fighting fish.

Fruit Flies

Also ordered through classified advertisements, vestigial winged fruit flies (*Drosophila*) can't fly but they can hop to great heights. Culture them in jars plugged with cotton. Like microworms, they feed on the yeast that grows on baby food paste, but commercial food mix may be enriched with corn syrup and corn flour; recipes abound. The white maggots climb and pupate on the glass walls or on folded paper towels inserted into the jars. The jar is tamped down vigorously to cause the flies to fall, then quickly uncapped and inverted to shake out the flies (without shaking out the food), and quickly restoppered. The harvested flies sprinkled on the surface of the water are greedily consumed by adult fish. Few cultured foods are as nutritious.

Dry Foods

The better commercial flake, pellet, and grain foods are mostly fish meal, rich in protein. Foods based on grains are mostly carbohydrate

Freeze-dried plankton.

and worthless for insectivorous fishes. The best foods are fortified with vitamins and *Spirulina* algae, but never as nutritious as live insects. You may see fish ravenously eat dry foods, but feeding can be induced by flavor enhancers (garlic, certain amino acids). Flake foods are convenient to purchase, store, and use, and add to the efficiency of large commercial operations. Fighting fish do well on flake foods supplemented with *Artemia*. Commercial trout chow may be the richest of granular foods for insectivorous fishes and is the cheapest.

Some high-quality dry food preparations are popular with *Betta* fanciers. BettaMin from Tetra is mostly fish meal and ground rice, supplemented with yeast, shrimp meal, algae meal, fish oils (a HUFA source), lecithin, and vitamin C. Betta Bio-Gold from Hikari is primarily shrimp meal (rich in HUFAs), fish meal, and yeast, supplemented with a broad array of vitamins, but no fish oils. If using dried foods as a staple, mix or alternate several to provide a varied diet.

Freeze-dried Foods

Freeze-dried krill (marine zooplankton) is a rich source of proteins, fats, carotenoids, and HUFAs. The dust particles can be fed to fry. Other freeze-dried foods have less nutritive value, and may spread disease because they are poorly cleaned of sewage bacteria before processing.

Paste Foods

Many breeders have favorite recipes for paste foods. The basic formula consists of beef heart, fish, or liver to make up the bulk of the preparation, supplemented with egg, shrimp, spinach, or liver, and enhanced with a multivitamin mixture, cod liver oil, lecithin, color enhancer (*Spirulina* blue-green algae or astaxanthin), and a gelatin binder. The meat is picked to remove tough fibers that can choke fish, and blended until smooth with the other ingredients and enough water to make the paste. It is then placed in plastic bags and laid flat in a freezer. As needed, a bag is opened and a piece of the blend broken off, thawed out, and fed to the fish. Variations include the addition of squid entrails, fish roe, insects, krill, and other rich sources of HUFAs.

A Word on Feeding

Feed once or twice a day an amount they can consume in five minutes. Dry food leftovers will decay, requiring partial water changes to maintain quality water. Fish crowded into grow-out tanks should be fed more frequently and receive more frequent water changes to remove wastes. Fish maintained in small jars are in even greater danger from bacterial decomposition and should have complete (100 percent) water changes weekly.

The feeding of live baby brine shrimp (nauplii), while exceptionally nutritious, presents risks. Salt added to the water will help the nauplii survive 24 hours or more, but they too eventually die in fresh water and will decay. When conducting water changes, remember to include the addition of one teaspoonful of marine salts per gallon of replacement water.

The foods resulting in least decay are *Daphnia* and tubifex or black worms. These live foods survive indefinitely in fresh water and enhance water quality. Tubifex worms and black worms eat decaying foods on the bottom

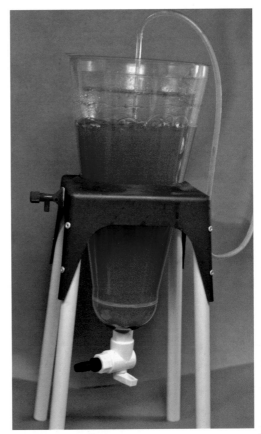

Hatching brine shrimp.

of the aquarium. *Daphnia* feed on algae, yeast, and bacteria. Aquatic live foods can be fed in sufficient quantity to maintain their populations in the breeding, grow-out, or fry tanks. They provide the best nutritive value, and are recommended if you plan to travel for a while. With excess live foods in a tank (except brine shrimp), fish are assured a steady food supply until you return.

COMMON DISEASES AND TREATMENTS

Parasites are normal in and on wild animals. Under ordinary circumstances they do little or no harm to their hosts, for to kill the host would be to end their own lives. Captivity changes all of that.

Every animal has parasites. Wild bettas (and other wild fishes) are hosts to creatures whose way of life requires another animal (and sometimes plant) for completion of the life cycle, from birth to reproduction before death. Just as a fish requires a stream, river, pond, or lake in which to live, feed, and reproduce, so a parasitic protozoan requires a fish on which to feed and perhaps reproduce, and provide it with transport from place to place.

Under conditions of crowding, the host becomes stressed and weakened, and its immune system, upon which it depends to counteract the adverse effects of parasites, becomes overworked and inefficient. Although the host may be capable of eating and breathing for itself and a small number of parasites, it cannot survive superinfections.

The parasites of wild bettas probably do little harm in nature, but in aquariums and ponds can multiply to cause superinfections. Aquarists

The beautiful Doubletail Blue Cambodia **(Betta splendens).**

should be aware of normal parasites on wild fish and conditions that favor diseases.

The principal causes of disease and death in fishes are temperature, chemicals, bacteria, protozoa, worms, and arthropods. In general, pet industry fish disease books are inadequate. For better information on fish diseases and treatments, consult a veterinary handbook such as Noga (2010). Breeders should take fish suffering from an outbreak of disease to a veterinarian for diagnosis and recommendations for treatment. The costs of the consultation and value of prescription medication will be more than offset by the time and livestock saved.

Environmental and Chemical Diseases
Temperature

Bettas are adapted to temperatures of 70°–90°F (21°–32°C). Higher temperatures reduce the oxygen-carrying capacity of water and induce stress from hypoxia, requiring dependence on the labyrinth. Colder temperatures depress the immune system, so normally harmless microorganisms can become pathogenic. Overall, bettas are more at risk from overheating than from cold temperatures. Faulty thermostats in aquarium heaters corrode and stick, resulting in continuous heating. Large-scale breeders heat the room rather than the tanks. For small-scale breeding and safety, it is better to undersize a heater. For example, if the recommended heater size is 5 watts per gallon, reduce that substantially. Then, if the thermostat sticks, the heater will be incapable of overheating the tank but still adequate to ameliorate chilling. An alternative is to replace heaters annually, so no heater is so old that it is a candidate for corrosion or sticking of the thermostat.

TIP

Preparation and Treatment of Tap Water

Major breeders of Siamese fighting fish fill a barrel with tap water and add sodium thiosulfate or ascorbic acid and aeration. After one or two days, the chlorine or chloramine has been neutralized and the supersaturated air has bubbled out of solution and dissipated. The aged, treated water, now at room temperature, is ready for any use required. Cover the barrel to keep out dust and oil. Because Siamese fighting fish have been domesticated for thousands of generations, these commercially available fish do not require the water conditions of their wild ancestors.

Chlorine

All tropical fishes are susceptible to the biocidal or killing effects of chlorine or chloramine in tap water. Chlorine is a volatile gas that evaporates in a few days. Chloramine is chlorine gas stabilized with ammonia and does not evaporate. Municipal water supplies are typically chlorinated in cold weather and chloraminated in warm weather. For safety's sake, always treat new water with a chemical dechlorinator from a pet store.

Air

If fish are placed in a tank with dechlorinated tap water within hours of removal from the tap, bubbles of air may appear on the glass and on the fish as the air comes out of supersaturated solution. More importantly, bubbles also occur on the gills of the fishes, causing the gill tissue to burn. A newly filled tank should rest for two days before adding fishes.

Infectious Diseases

Bacteria

Bacteria vary from primitive forms associated with deep-sea vents to the highly specialized forms related to algae and fungi and today classified as blue-greens or cyanobacteria. Most bacteria are helpful. Some aerobically oxidize toxic ammonia to less toxic nitrite, some oxidize nitrite to harmless nitrate, and some anaerobically reduce nitrate to nitrogen and oxygen gases. Bacteria in the intestine make essential vitamins, but also include pathogens. A pathogen causes disease. When we refer to bacteria as pathogenic, we mean capable of causing a serious disease.

Of the pathogenic (disease-causing) bacteria, most have one characteristic in common, a red reaction to the Gram stain procedure used in bacteriological laboratories. This red reaction (really a negative reaction to a purple stain leaving only the underlying red stain visible) is called a Gram-negative reaction, whereas a bacterium that stains purple is said to be Gram positive. Gram-negative and Gram-positive bacteria have two different cell wall structures.

Treatments

Chemicals synthesized in the laboratory (such as sulfa drugs) are called antimicrobials. Chemicals produced by other microbes are called antibiotics.

Most antibiotics and antimicrobials kill bacteria in water, the gut, the blood, or the lymph. Once inside the host fish's cells, the bacteria may be resistant to treatment.

Many antibiotics target either Gram-positive bacteria (such as penicillin or erythromycin on *Renibacterium*) or Gram-negative bacteria (such as oxytetracycline on *Aeromonas* and *Flexibacter*). Ignore brand or trade names and read the label on the package. With rare exceptions, the bacteria pathogenic to tropical fishes are all Gram negative. Medicaments whose principal ingredient is erythromycin are ineffective against Gram-negative disease-causing bacteria and kill valuable Gram-positive nitrogen-cycle bacteria.

An effective medicament for *Aeromonas* and other common Gram-negative bacteria is nifurpirinol (Furanace, Furazolidone), which is absorbed by the fish from water, but cannot be used in food. One dose of 2 mg/gallon for six hours may be sufficient. Treat in dim light or darkness, as the drug breaks down in bright light.

Flexibacter *infection.*

The quinolones (oxolinic acid derivatives) are broad-spectrum antibiotics effective against Gram-positive and Gram-negative bacteria, and can be applied in water at 40 mg/gal for 24 hours. Water application (bath) should only be used in a bare container and never in a community tank. Fluoroquinolones such as sarafloxacin are used in dry feed or by medicating brine shrimp to carry the drug.

Cotton wool disease. The most common cause of sudden mass mortalities of adult bettas is cotton wool disease. It is an infection of the epithelium (outer skin), produced by the Gram-negative rod-shaped bacterium, *Flexibacter columnaris* and its relatives. The bacteria are ubiquitous in water and on fishes, but usually cause disease outbreaks in fish that have been recently stressed by, for example, shipping, low temperature, low oxygen, or crowding. Cotton wool disease begins as a translucent mucoid

Betta *with fin rot.*

layer on the skin that rapidly expands, eating away the flesh and leaving the muscle and blood vessels exposed. Within hours a wispy exudate or pus emerges from the lesion into the water column. That exudate is a solid mass of filamentous bacteria multiplying so fast that they spread out of the fish and into the water.

Management requires isolating each fish and discarding those with advanced lesions because they are too far gone. Fishes with early stage lesions should be placed in clean water with potassium permanganate following package directions. Uninfected fish from the same batch (source, shipment) should be treated as a prophylactic measure. Sulfa drugs applied to the wound have also been recommended.

Bloat. Bloat is typically an advanced (untreatable) bacterial infection of the blood stream resulting from a gut blockage with the principal symptom of a distended abdomen caused by fluid accumulation in all the tissues and the body cavity. It is accompanied by disorientation, lethargy, and inevitably death. Swelling of the abdomen similar to bloat may

occur with roundworms in the intestine, but the fish is active, roundworms or their egg-laden slime poke out from the vent, it's not rapidly contagious, and the disease can be treated with fenbendazole-medicated food. Sometimes swelling of the abdomen is caused by masses of flagellated protozoans, a condition that spreads through the tank, but is treatable with metronidazole-medicated food. Medicated fish foods are available from pet stores or on-line.

Fin and Tail Rot. Fin and tail rot may be caused by *Aeromonas* and *Pseudomonas* in fishes stressed by crowding, decomposing food in the aquarium, or fluctuating temperatures. The fins become brown or darkened at their eroded margins. Change water, add Melafix and one teaspoonful of marine salts per 5 gallons (19 L), do not feed any dry foods, increase aeration, reduce the light, and raise the temperature to about 85°F (29°C). Potassium permanganate sometimes helps, but may burn (oxidize) the gills. A 25-percent water change with *underchlorinated* tap water may help, because mild chlorine exposure can lower the microbe population without reaching a toxic level to fish. Don't try this in the summer when tap water is likely to contain chloramines.

"Pop Eye." "Pop eye," or exophthalmos, without septicemia indicates a localized bacterial infection of the sinuses. The bacteria in the epithelial linings in the head produce gases that force the eyeball outward. The only treatment is gram-negative antibiotics in food, and it doesn't always work. Many kinds of bacteria produce gas, and most can reach the eye if infections proceed to septicemia. If the fish doesn't die within a week, it is likely to live.

Vibrios. The genus *Vibrio* contains the comma-shaped bacteria causing cholera and other diseases. Vibrios have been associated with human deaths after eating or being cut by oysters, and with necrotic diseases requiring amputations to save a life. They can cause freshwater and marine fish diseases. Many bettas are collected from near brackish habitats similar to North American habitats in which vibrios are found, and vibrios might come in with wild fish. They can be killed by Gram-negative antibiotics, but the fish must be treated promptly.

Acid-fast disease. Another staining reaction, the Acid Fast stain, is used in medical laboratories to detect that group of bacteria, known as *Mycobacteria*, that cause tuberculosis, leprosy, and other important diseases. These bacteria have wax-laden walls that render them resistant to most antibiotics used to eliminate Gram-negative and Gram-positive bacteria. A complicating factor is that most mycobacteria (or acid-fast bacteria) grow slowly so medicaments take a long time to work.

Mycobacterial infections are associated with impaired immune systems associated with old age. Fishes long past their prime, those raised at high temperatures, and fishes known to be old compared with their relatives are often victims. Infections manifest as slow-growing bloody lesions anywhere on the body. Diagnosis is confirmed by red-stained rods in a skin smear treated with the acid fast-staining technique. The lesions don't respond to antibiotic treatments. There are no cost-effective treatments. Affected fish are discarded or quarantined until they die. Acid-fast bacteria are not particularly contagious.

Betta with abdominal swelling, later confirmed to be Mycobacterium infection.

Protozoa

Velvet disease. Perhaps no disease is less recognized and more important than the dino-flagellate causing velvet disease, *Piscinoodinium. Piscinoodinium* is related to both animals and plants, sometimes included in the protozoa (as here) and sometimes to the pathogenic algae. It is related to the red tide group of marine dinoflagellates. Both domestic and wild bettas are susceptible.

Velvet flourishes where water quality has declined. It is the single most important killer of fry of *Betta splendens* and few other species seem resistant. When excess food decomposes, bacteria release waste acids. The weakened fry are easy prey for *Piscinoodinium*. The dinoflagellate spreads through air droplets. It probably exists in all aquariums. The infection appears as a dusty golden layer over the body and eyes, best seen by light glancing off the flanks. Use a flashlight after dark for best visualization.

Piscinoodinium invades the epithelium. A healthy fish can withstand a heavy infection for weeks. *Piscinoodinium* can be treated with copper sulfate or formalin. Flubendazole

Coelomic swelling due to mycobacteriosis.

powder sprinkled on the water surface will kill *Piscinoodinium*.

Most losses of fry are caused by velvet invading the skin of newborn bettas. Velvet can be kept at bay by maintaining high water quality (siphoning detritus and debris from the bottom of the fry tank), and maintaining a salt concentration of one teaspoon per gallon to assist gill function and osmotic balance. Once a batch of fry is infected, the few survivors will be so weak they may develop poorly or could be deformed or stunted.

White spot disease or ich. The most common protozoan disease of freshwater tropical fish is infection of the skin by *Ichthyophthirius multifilis*. This parasitic ciliate is ubiquitous in natural waters and causes epidemics when fishes are stressed and their immune defenses are lowered, as by cold temperatures. Ich is a common springtime disease of pond fishes and, because many aquarium fishes are produced in ponds in Florida, it is most common in pet stores in the spring. It probably occurs in all aquari-

ums where it remains dormant until the fish are stressed or a new fish is introduced to the tank. Fish that recover from ich seldom become seriously infested again, but can be carriers.

The disease manifests as a few small white spots on the body or fins. After several days to a week, the number and the size of the spots increase dramatically. In the ich life cycle, a young protozoan penetrates and infects the skin and then grows to a large size. This feeding stage or trophont (troph=to feed) is the white spot, and it can attain the size of a pinhead. At maturity, the trophont encysts and breaks out of the skin, where it drifts until it sticks to the gravel, rocks, or plants. (In severe cases, the lesions in the skin become infected with bacteria and the fish die of bacterial septicemia.) The stage inside the cyst, called a tomont, divides repeatedly to produce perhaps a thousand offspring. When fully developed, the infective theronts break out of the cyst and swim about seeking to infect more (or the original) fish. Stressed, crowded fish are readily invaded. Once they burrow into the skin, they become trophonts and the cycle continues.

While in the skin, the protozoan cannot be reached by chemicals. Outside the skin within its cyst, it is protected from chemicals by the cyst wall. Only when the infective parasites break out of the cyst and swim through water are they susceptible to formalin, malachite green, metronidazole, copper sulfate or chloroquine. Quick-Cure is formalin and malachite green. Treatment consists of maintaining any of these chemicals in the water for a protracted period in order to be effective when the cysts hatch. Raise the aquarium temperature to shorten cyst development time and simultaneously boost the fishes' immune systems.

Immunity

Fishes resist disease by physical barriers (skin and scales), engulfing white blood cells (phagocytes), and another group of white blood cells that release antibodies and their helpers.

White cells are of many kinds with different metabolisms. They all take up nutrients and secrete waste products. One group of them, however, secretes other substances called antibodies and cytokinins.

The best known white cells (phagocytes) are attached to blood vessels and the liver. Other phagocytes move freely inside and outside the blood and lymph vessels. It's their job to catch both passing alien materials like bacteria, viruses, fungi, and dead tissues, or even travel through the body looking for them. Whether they trap them or pounce on them, they then engulf and digest these aliens rendering them dead and harmless. The accumulations of traveling white cells you see at wounds are called pus.

The antibodies and cytokinins are produced by another group of white cells found only in the blood stream. When these cells (called CD8 or T-cells) contact a new alien substance, they change to alter their secretions to a mirror of a piece of the alien; this secretion is the antibody. The mutated cells then proliferate and secrete large amounts of antibodies that tag the alien and expose it to attack by two kinds of other white cells—those that emit cytokinins (poisons) and those that eat the tagged alien. Fish are not very efficient the first time they encounter an invader, but become more efficient next time.

BREEDING BETTAS

Most people breed bettas in a small aquarium and move the fry to larger tanks as they grow. I prefer to start with a larger tank.

Males housed in individual jars are ready to spawn when they build a higher-than-usual bubblenest, often triggered by a water change. Females are ready to spawn when the abdomen is full and rounded, the white ovipositor (the protruding spot at the end of the oviduct) becomes prominent, and the horizontal dark lines on the body change to vertical dark bands on a light background. Banding is difficult to see on densely pigmented fish.

The breeding aquarium is usually a 2- to 10-gallon tank filled with dechlorinated tap water of pH 6.8–7.2, and warmed from an ambient temperature in the low to middle 70s°F/24°C to a breeding temperature in the low 80s°F/27–28°C. It's a good idea to add one teaspoonful of noniodized salt or marine salts per gallon of water to assist the gills in maintaining osmotic balance. If you use a larger tank, fill it to a water level of 6 inches. Cover the tank to keep out dust and airborne oil, and illuminate it with an aquarium reflector, window, or lamp light. Add a styrofoam cup cut lengthwise in half or floating plants (*Ceratopteris, Ceratophyllum, Salvinia*, a large leaf from a tree) to provide support for the nest. Add a flowerpot or submerged vegetation (*Vesicularia, Nitella*) as a refuge. Use a bare-bottom tank for ease of cleaning.

Introducing the Male

Float the jar containing the male in cooler water into the warmer breeding aquarium for an hour to warm up. Then gently spill the male into the tank and remove the jar. The male is held alone until he builds a bubblenest, often the first day, and almost always within three days. If he doesn't build a nest, place a jar with a female or even another male next to the tank to induce nest construction.

Introducing the Female

Place a jar containing the female inside the breeding tank; its water level should exceed that of the tank so that it is heavy enough to sit firmly on the bottom. The elevated temperature and sight of the male trigger her mature eggs to ripen for breeding.

The male displays to the female by erecting his fins and undulating his body as he swims

Bubblenesting male.

Bettas *spawning.*

back and forth or rushes forward as though to bite through the jar. He alternates displaying with attending his bubblenest, increasing its breadth and height.

If the female displays horizontal lines, ignores the male, is thin, or fails to display a prominent white oviduct spot, she is not ready to spawn. She is ready when she vigorously attempts to break out of the jar and reach the male, her bold vertical dark bands become enhanced, and the white oviduct spot is prominent. After two or three days, tip her into the tank with the male.

The male will become excited, rapidly darting around her, fins spread and body undulating. He attempts to drive her under the nest, but may kill her if she does not accept his advances. With a larger (10-gallon) tank and a refuge, she is unlikely to be killed.

Spawning

After numerous false starts, the female follows the male to the nest and butts his flank as he curves his body into a tight U around her, ventral surfaces apposed. They tremble for a few seconds and suddenly freeze, slowly sinking immobile as a stream of opaque white eggs spills from the embrace and precedes their slow descent. The freeze was the moment of orgasm. The sinking eggs carry his sperm adherent to their surfaces, and the nuclei of both parents will fuse within minutes to create the new zygotes.

Spitting eggs.

The male recovers first and swims downward to catch the eggs before they reach the floor of the aquarium. He will pick few off the bottom. Males vary greatly, some not accepting eggs from the floor, others not recovering from orgasm until all the eggs have reached the floor and then picking them up or ignoring them entirely. Usually the male picks up all the eggs he can catch in midwater and approaches the bubblenest, his mouth working in a chewing motion. At the nest he expels the eggs upward in a cloud of sticky bubbles from below. Most of the eggs stick to the bottom of the bubblenest and are easy to see with a flashlight as opaque white dots on a glassy surface.

The female recovers after the male, and seems interested only in eating eggs she can catch on the way down or from the floor.

Within minutes, they repeat the routine, and continue spawning for an hour or more, producing 100 to 400 eggs. A complete spawning event averages 50 to 60 embraces, each yielding one to 15 eggs. Lucas reported up to 1,421 eggs from a single spawn.

After the female is spent, she attempts to hide. She may not be noticeably thinner, her ovipositor will still be apparent, and her markings may not change, so she may still be excited but have no more fully ripe eggs. The male is never spent and will harass the female when she stops spawning. She should now be removed and isolated for recovery at

the same elevated temperature. Females suddenly stressed by colder water after the stress of spawning may develop infections of bite wounds. Maintaining them for a few days at 80°F/27°C aids their immune systems in protecting them from wound infections.

Now the male spends all his time reinforcing his nest, adding and replacing bubbles, slurp-

Falling eggs.

A bubblenest.

ing up the eggs for cleaning by rolling them around his mouth in saliva, and then spitting them back under the nest. Rarely are males egg-eaters.

At 24 hours, the eggs begin to hatch releasing the nonfeeding, barely developed prolarvae sticking to the bubble nest. If you shine a light from below, you will see tiny tails pointing straight downward and now know that both fish were fertile. The male continues blowing bubbles in profusion, the mucus protecting the newly hatched fry from diseases and microscopic predators and grazers. The fry apparently are now supported within the nest by cement glands on the head rather than by bubble mucus, as they are always oriented tail down.

In another day, the white prolarvae darken as they develop into larvae, and begin dropping from the nest, then darting back up on their own. At this time the male's assistance drops off, and he may wander away explor-

ing for food. A day later the larvae (fry) swim horizontally and begin searching for food. Now you can remove the male to a jar for recovery and, like the female, slowly acclimate it back to ambient room temperature.

Care of the Fry

Weeks One and Two

After you remove the male, replace the tank cover with plastic food wrap taped in place. Plastic wrap is better than glass in providing a tight seal in which the air above the nest and water is maintained at high humidity and at approximately the same temperature as the water. The warm humid atmosphere is helpful to development of the delicate labyrinth during the next three weeks. If the air is cold or dry, the developing cells do not grow well, and the raw exposed tissue may become infected.

When the fry begin darting near the surface, they should be fed infusoria (rotifer, ciliate) culture. The next day they swim at all levels of the aquarium (free swimming). Increase the infusoria, but not so much that the water clouds. If you have green water, add this as well.

Several slurry and powdered fry foods on the market are accepted by fry, but not readily, and the uneaten residue risks bacterial blooms that degrade water quality and induce velvet outbreaks. The benefits of synthetic foods are mostly their ability to grow bacteria that in turn induce blooms of protozoa. I consider these foods dangerous and recommend against their use unless you have nothing else available.

The next day, begin feeding newly hatched *Artemia* nauplii. Only a few fry will take nauplii this early, indicated by their stomachs swelling orange from shrimp instead of white from infusoria. In addition to nauplii, continue feeding infusoria for at least another week.

Some breeders omit infusoria and feed brine shrimp nauplii from the beginning. Only the largest fry survive. The result is smaller spawns raised, but more robust fish. Presumably, after a number of generations, the average size of fry has increased.

Don't be concerned if your fry do not adhere to this schedule. Development is temperature dependent, so slightly cooler water will extend the time to each stage by a day or so, and warmer water may speed it up.

Week Three: Grow-out

At three weeks, the fry are miniatures of the adults and consume much more food. Nitrate wastes build up and can stunt growth. Now the fry are strong enough to be transferred to a grow-out tank for heavier feedings and regular cleaning without fear of siphoning out the young. Set the small breeding tank inside the larger grow-out tank for 24 hours of temperature equilibration. Then tip the smaller into the larger slowly, and slosh the final small amount from the corner where fry invariably accumulate. Remove the breeding tank for cleaning and reuse. The next day, top off the tank by placing a bucket of new water above the tank, and siphoning it downward through tubing. The slow flow through the tube minimizes temperature changes. Keep the tank covered with plastic wrap to protect the water surface from oil and dust.

A 10- or 20-gallon tank is fine for initial grow-out. A combination of water changes and nutritious feeding (especially *Artemia* nauplii) produces rapid growth, and not food alone.

Fish wastes generate growth-inhibiting nitrites and nitrates, best removed by water changes.

Within two months, the labyrinth is developed, and the young are ready for transfer to larger quarters (females and indeterminate fish) or separation into individual jars for final growth. In small tanks the young grow unevenly. The largest fish should be constantly moved to other quarters to keep them from starving out or eating the others. More even growth occurs in large grow-out tanks (55 gallons) where growth inhibitors do not suddenly reach high concentrations. When the young males begin showing aggression, remove them to individual jars where they can grow without fin damage to themselves or other males. You can house females together in a single tank.

Tips

The key to raising healthy fry is maximizing water volume, which maintains water quality by providing maximum space for babies, live foods, bacteria, and dilution of waste products. Good water quality is critical to keeping the fry resistant to velvet disease, the most important killer of baby fish. Healthy fry can resist velvet.

Ken Muller found that leaving the female with the male after spawning (with abundant vegetation for a refuge), encouraged nest protecting behavior. Furthermore, when leaving the female and male permanently in the aquarium even after the fry were free-swimming, the parents did not eat all the fry, and continued to produce several spawns with the fry of earlier spawns in the aquarium. Bettas raised in this manner seemed to produce kinder, gentler breeders in the next generation, with lowered aggression and fin damage during spawning.

HOW-TO: SHIPPING BETTAS

Joining any of the clubs specializing in fancy Siamese fighting fish (*Betta splendens*) or wild bettas (mouthbrooders and other bubblenesters) will quickly introduce you to the plethora of species and strains only available from other specialists. You won't see them in pet stores and, unless you are ready to receive (and later send) fish via air transportation, you will be missing a large part of the world of the species of *Betta*. However, you can't just put a fish in a plastic bag and mail it elsewhere.

Packing

Bettas should be packed in individual plastic bags. The bag should be filled to one third or less of its volume with water and two thirds or more of its volume with air. The bag is sealed with two rubber bands (one as a backup). For small quantities, this bag is then inverted into another bag, and it too sealed with rubber bands. Inversion of the one bag into another obliterates corners that can trap the fish. For large quantities, many small bags are then placed inside one large bag as backup in case of leakage.

Preparation for Packing

Fish fed today will excrete and defecate tomorrow, and sometimes the day after. To prepare fish for shipping, place them in a clean container of new water and starve them for two days. This period will be sufficient for them to purge their intestinal tracts so that they do not purge while in transit.

Shipping Unpurged Fish

Failure to purge fish prior to shipping will result in defecation in the sealed plastic bag, decomposition of the fecal wastes by bacteria leading to acidification and deoxygenation of the water, a build-up of ammonia, and risk of death. The water in the bag containing the dead fish will be milky and foul-smelling.

Carriers

The U.S. Postal Service will accept live fish. Priority mail typically takes two to three days, an acceptable period for fish with a large volume of air in the bag. Despite advertising overnight or two-day guaranteed delivery, I have never had an Express Mail package arrive alive and in less than a week. Federal Express accepts fish, but United Parcel Service does not. Many airlines reject packages labeled live fish. Labels can be counterproductive, and I have stopped marking my packages as containing live fish. I use everything but Express Mail.

Temperature

Fishes should be transported only during periods of moderate weather. Winter and midsummer shipments are risky. Heat packs provide warmth for less than 24 hours and have limited value. Heat packs should be taped to the box lid.

Boxes

The ideal shipping container is a picnic cooler, but most aquarists use styrofoam boxes within cardboard boxes. All empty space is filled with packing peanuts, bubblewrap, or shredded paper.

Breathing Bags

One type of fish bag permits the diffusion of oxygen and carbon dioxide across the plastic membrane while retaining water. Kordon's Breathing Bags must be special ordered in quantity and are popular for shipping all kinds of fishes that lack sharp spines. An ordinary

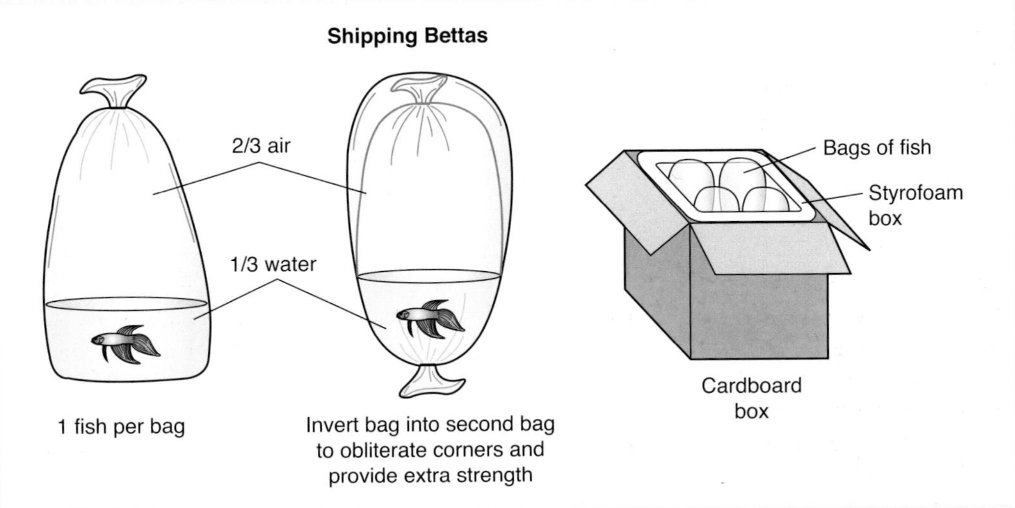

Shipping Bettas

2/3 air

1/3 water

1 fish per bag

Invert bag into second bag
to obliterate corners and
provide extra strength

Bags of fish

Styrofoam
box

Cardboard
box

plastic fish shipping bag contains enough sealed-in oxygen and void space above the water to support a fish for up to three days. Breathing bags can support fish for more than a week because carbon dioxide leaves across the plastic membrane and oxygen constantly enters. When fish finally die in a breathing bag, it is because of starvation rather than bad air. Breathing bags must be used correctly. All air must be expelled so all portions of the membrane are in contact with water. Fish need to be less crowded. If you normally pack one fish in a half cup of water, you now need to pack one fish in a cup of water, and so on. When the bags are packed for shipment, they must not contact one another, for contact would prevent gas exchange. Each bag is separated from all other bags with cardboard, newspaper, or (for tourists bringing back fish from a foreign land), dirty clothes in a suitcase. As with ordinary shipping bags, the fish must be purged prior to packing; otherwise, fecal matter or regurgitated food will lead to decomposition that degrades the water.

LARGE-SCALE PRODUCTION

The commercial production of blue gouramies (Cole et al., 1997) offers ideas for the aquarist contemplating large-scale production of bettas. The two species are related, have similar needs and breeding behavior, and their responses to care and treatment are probably similar.

Vitellogenesis (Yolk Development)

Because egg development and production occurs in discrete stages, a number of steps condition the brood stock. Ovarian egg development proceeds through several stages before the eggs acquire yolk (vitellogenesis) and more stages before the eggs ripen and are capable of being fertilized. Vitellogenesis is induced by the visual cues of males building bubblenests. During bubblenest construction, the males release chemicals called steroid glucuronides. These chemicals stimulate the vitellogenic (yolk stage) eggs to swell and ripen. That means that the female will undergo vitellogenesis in the jar, but her eggs won't ripen until she is tipped into the same water as the male and exposed to his chemicals.

Betta splendens *with half moon tail.*

There is a direct correlation between body weight of parental males and females and the number of fry they produce, a correlation between number of fry and size of the nest, but no correlation between nest size and parent size. The best spawns are from the largest males with the largest bubblenests. But even a small male can produce a large nest.

Males can detect females with ripe eggs by the odoriferous chemicals (pheromones) the females release into the water. Males do not respond to females with unripe eggs. Females constantly produce new batches of eggs and can be spawned every two weeks. Ripe females not allowed to spawn may spontaneously release their overripe eggs, which quickly decompose as indicated by an oily sheen on the water.

Reducing light by providing shading reinforces breeding behavior (Degani, 1989). Low light results in slower (several days) but more frequent spawns, and higher light levels result in faster spawning (within two days). Low temperatures retard spawning behavior, and very low temperatures are lethal. The same wide range of moderate temperatures are acceptable for conditioning and for spawning, and conditioned fish do not need an increased temperature to induce spawning, although light reduction through plant shading might stimulate spawning.

Fish are conditioned for two weeks prior to spawning. During this time they are fed live or frozen food (black worms, tubifex worms, bloodworms), a paste food (made from beef heart and liver mixed with peas and spinach), and a dry food of not less than 32 percent protein.

After conditioning, each male is placed in a breeding tank early in the morning to acclimate and establish a territory. The breeding tank should be dimly lit with little foot traffic to avoid disturbing the pairs. Males often begin bubblenest construction within three hours. A floating substratum for the bubblenest is added, such as a floating plant or a half of a Styrofoam cup.

Spawning should occur in one to four days. Afterward the female is removed to prevent further injury. The eggs hatch in 24 hours at 80°F/27°C and remain in the nest for the next two or three days while the yolk is resorbed. At day 4 or 5, the fry are free swimming (horizontal) below the nest but weak swimmers. When they are strong swimmers, feeding is initiated, and the male is removed.

Care of the Fry

If the fish have been spawned in small containers, the fry need to be moved. This is accomplished by siphoning the water out until only one inch remains in the breeding tank and the fry are concentrated in a small volume. Fry transfers are done in the early morning under dim light to avoid photic shock and because the variation in temperatures of different containers should be minimal; temperature variation will be greater later in the day from uneven exposure to sunlight and other heat sources.

Fry fed protozoa or infusoria grow better than fry fed artificial diets or egg yolk-yeast mixtures, either because the infusoria are more nutritious or, more likely, because living foods do not contribute to leftover waste that supports bacterial decomposition leading to a drop in pH and rise in growth-inhibiting nitrites (Degani, 1990).

The entire container is set inside the grow-out tank or pond with as little sloshing as possible, and water from the larger container is added to the smaller in small increments to minimize temperature shock.

Once the fry are acclimated by addition of grow-out tank water, the smaller container is gently tipped and removed with as little turbulence as possible. It is now time to feed the fry in the grow-out tank.

The grow-out tank has been prepared seven to 10 days before, starting with the addition of a commercial 10-30-0 liquid fertilizer and an algal culture. In a few days under bright light, the tank has grown an algal bloom. After the water becomes green with algae, it is seeded with *Daphnia* or with the freshwater rotifers *Brachionus calcyflorus* or *B. rubens*. When the *Daphnia* or *Brachionus* have grown out large populations (bloomed), using up much of the algae, the tank is ready to receive the baby fish. If the blooms fail to develop, the fish are instead fed a preparation of microencapsulated commercial feed or artificial plankton (APR or artificial plankton-rotifer). The dry preparation is mixed with water until thoroughly wetted, and then sprayed over the surface of the grow-out tank or pond every other day. The fry are also fed two or three times a day with newly hatched *Artemia* nauplii and a commercial dry food until day 10, at which time they are weaned off *Artemia* and fed dry food exclusively. (High-quality fish such as bettas may be fed frozen adult *Artemia* and meaty paste foods.)

In commercial pond grow-out facilities, a sample of the population is measured and weighed to calculate the weight of the entire population. The amount of food per feeding is then calculated based on total fish weight. Furthermore, because color intensity has value, fish farms purchase and use commercial feeds supplemented with color enhancers such as beta carotene, canthaxanthin, astaxanthin, and xanthophyll. Canthaxanthin also increases iridescence. Color enhancers usually make up 0.05 percent active ingredient in the dry food.

Commercial diets were found to be just as effective as egg yolk and yeast. Growth rates varied little with different diets. Water quality was more important than diet in controlling growth. Increased nitrite is the most important growth inhibitor.

(Optimal water quality for mass production and high growth rates are unrelated to water quality of the species in the wild. In fact, many fish occur in particular habitats not because those are the best conditions, but because the fish can survive these conditions whereas their competitors or predators cannot.)

At low stocking densities, growth is almost uniform. At high stocking densities, growth is uneven and slows. The highest growth rate is attained with low stocking densities, frequent water changes, and aeration.

In pond culture, weeds are managed with herbicides a month before harvest. A week before harvest, some of the fish are removed and inspected for parasites or diseases. If treatment is required, the pond is treated. The fish are sampled again and if necessary treated again before harvest. Harvesting is accomplished with seines, the hauls kept small and numerous to prevent crushing of the fish by too many in the net at a time.

After harvest the fish are placed in acclimation aquariums with clean water for observation to detect injuries, for adjustment to smaller quarters, and for sorting. Salt is added at 9 parts per thousand (ppt), which is isotonic (the same salinity as fish blood). This reduces stress and stimulates a normal protective slime coat. Damaged or otherwise unmarketable fish are discarded. A holding period before bagging and shipping allows time for the fish to purge their intestinal tracts so they will not purge them in the shipping bags where bacterial decomposition of fecal waste and regurgitated food will degrade water quality and consume oxygen.

Fish are often anaesthetized before bagging with quinaldine or with tricaine methanesulfonate (MS-222), and treated with a synthetic slime that helps reduce injuries.

BETTA GENETICS

Generally, a trait is controlled by a gene made of DNA. Every individual has hundreds of thousands of gene pairs, one gene of each pair from each parent. Genes control the production of enzymes and other proteins that determine how large fish get, coloration, susceptibility to a particular disease, and myriad other characteristics.

All the genes that make up a species or population is called the genome. Although we don't know the entire genome of *Betta splendens*, we know about some genes that control color and finnage. And we can use that information to set up a breeding program.

Betta Genetics 101: An Introduction

Let's say we have a strain of bettas in which 100 percent of the offspring are always long-finned. We will assume that fin length is controlled by one gene, and each parent has a pair of genes for long fins. We can illustrate the gene as L, and a pair of them (in the parent) as LL.

Doubletails, singletails, reds, yellows, greens, cambodias, and so on, are the visible manifestation of genes that control the way the fish develop. What the fish looks like is called its phenotype. It is not the same as the genes the fish actually carries, because some genes are masked by other genes.

Super half moon red **Betta splendens.**

Suppose we bred a longfinned betta with a shortfinned betta, and all of the offspring had long fins. It can happen if the gene for long fins (L) dominates the same chemical pathway coded by the gene for short fins. The two genes influence the same character and either compete or they work together. Both are on identical locations (*loci*, singular *locus*) on the same chromosome pair. Genes equivalent in location that act on the same character are called *alleles*. The genes for long fins and for short fins are alleles. If the longfin gene overwhelms the effect of the shortfin gene (i.e., is dominant to it), we symbolize the dominant gene as L and the recessive gene as l, indicating that long masks short. There is no way, just looking, that you could tell a pure longfin (LL) fish from one in which one parent was pure longfinned and one was a mixed longfin (Ll) as both would have long fins. The invisible genetic makeup is called the *genotype*, and it is what the fish is made of rather than what it looks like (the *phenotype*). For this particular pair of alleles, the genotype is LL, ll, or Ll, and the phenotype is longfinned or shortfinned.

There are other ways to symbolize genes, such as + for the wild type condition, whether it is dominant or recessive to the mutant condition. We can still use a capital letter for a gene that is dominant to the wild type gene, and a small letter for a gene recessive to the wild type gene.

An easy way to visualize the relationships between phenotypes and genotypes for any one trait is based on a mathematical box called a Punnet Square. Let's use fin length as an example. We know that long fins (the mutant condition) is dominant to the wild type condition of short fins. On one side of the box we put the two possible genes for the trait from one parent, and then the possible equivalent genes from the other parent. Each parent's eggs or sperm cells will contain only one gene of its original paired condition for fin length.

For the pure breeding longfinned strain, we write:

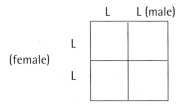

When an egg combines with a sperm, the only possible combinations are:

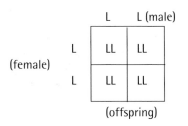

(offspring)

The pure longfinned male crossed with pure longfinned female will yield offspring that are both genotypically and phenotypically longfinned.

Now let's cross a longfinned male with a shortfinned female. We know that longfinned is dominant to shortfinned. If L represents the dominant longfinned gene, we can use a small letter (l) for the recessive trait.

	L	L (male)
l	Ll	Ll
l	Ll	Ll

(female)

Here the offspring appear (phenotypically) longfinned, but genotypically they are a combination of L and l. When two genes are identical as in LL, the fish is said to be *homozygous* for that gene (homo = the same). When they are different as in Ll, they are said to be *heterozygous* for that gene (hetero = different).

Let's say someone gave you a pair of longfinned fish but you did not know if they were Ll or LL. If they were LL, 100 percent of the offspring would be longfinned (LL). If both parents were Ll, then you would get about three longfinned to every shortfinned fish. How did I know that? Let's put those genes in a Punnet Square.

	L	l (male)
L	LL	Ll
l	Ll	ll

(female)

Green metallic half moon male
Betta splendens.

You can see that this cross would produce three longfinned fish (25 percent LL, 50 percent LI) to one shortfinned fish (25 percent II).

In the case above, the longfinned mutant is dominant to the wild type shortfinned condition. We could have used the plus symbol (+) for the wild type, and capital and small letters for dominant and recessive alleles of the wild type. In the preceding example, we would have written long fins as L and the wild type short fins as +. Using that symbolism, we would write L+ for the genotypically heterozygous fish with phenotypic long fins, ++ for the homozygous fish with phenotypic short fins (the wild type), and LL for the genotypically homozygous but phenotypically longfinned mutant.

Let's look at colors in bettas. We already understand dominance and recessiveness. Another condition is called incomplete dominance or blending. For this concept, you need to understand what is meant by cornflower blue and steel blue, and to do that we must first talk about green.

The phenotypic color green results from two identical genes for green coloration. The steel blue results from two identical genes for blue color. The cornflower blue betta is a mix of the blue and green genes. Steel blue is used for homozygous blue (BB). The same applies to the mixture of the blue and green genes called cornflower blue. Now let's see what happens when two genes blend.

Some genes are equal, resulting in incomplete dominance or blending of their coded traits. In this case we'll designate the allele for green color as G and that for blue as B. The

---

TIP

Predictive Value of the Punnet Square

You can use a Punnet Square to predict proportions for any character controlled by a single pair of alleles. The parents could be brother and sister, father and daughter, mother and son, cousins, or completely unrelated. What matters is whether the traits are controlled by one set of alleles, whether these alleles are dominant or recessive to each other, or whether they are not alleles at all. If the genes are on different loci, they are unrelated and a single gene Punnet Square box will not be predictive of the outcome. Conversely, if you don't get a ratio predicted by a Punnet Square, then more than one pair of genes is responsible for the character.

combination GB produces the cornflower blue phenotype.

		G	G (green male)
(steel	B	GB	GB
blue			
female)	B	GB	GB

Here 100 percent of the offspring are cornflower blue phenotypes but genotypically they are heterozygous for blue and green (genotype GB). There is a melding of colors to produce a new color typical of the heterozygote. Suppose you want to do this again but have no more steel blue or green breeding stock? Simply breed the cornflower blue brother to sister and you will regenerate the parental phenotypes.

		(cornflower blue male)	
		G	B
(cornflower	G	GG	GB
blue			
female)	B	GB	BB

The offspring are 25 percent green (GG), 25 percent steel blue (BB), and 50 percent cornflower blue (GB). In this example, every green or steel blue betta is a pure homozygous fish, and every cornflower blue fish is a heterozygote for the blue and green alleles.

Betta Genes: Fins

Wild *Betta splendens* have short fins and dermal pigments that include red pterins, red and yellow xanthins, black and brown melanins, and green iridocytes in the scales containing iridescent crystals of guanine. In most animals the wild type is dominant to almost all mutations, but that's not the rule in bettas.

The mutation of long fins is dominant to the wild type short fin state. The reason wild bettas don't all have long fins is because that extra finnage slows the fish down and makes it easy prey and an inefficient fighter. In nature, longfinned bettas don't survive for the same reason albinos don't survive to pass on their genes—they're a quick lunch.

Doubletail is a recessive finnage mutation. We indicate the homozygote as dt (there is no rule against using more than a single letter for a mutation) and the wild type or normal condition as + or DT.

Another mutation is fin rays protruding beyond the fin membrane to produce a combtail or fringed betta. This seems to be recessive to normal, whether the fish is longfinned or shortfinned.

Fringed orange doublefin Betta.

Betta Genes: Colors

Normal red can result from pterin pigments in pteridophores or from astaxanthin in xanthophores. The red pigment can cover the body, and all or only part of the fins (butterfly). A completely red (body and fins) betta is dominant over limited red (as in cambodia); the noncambodia red gene is called *extended red,* and its origin may be more than one set of alleles. The two mutants called *nonred* are xanthic (yellow) bettas resulting from the loss of red astaxanthin pigment and red pterin pigment, or the loss of one or both combined with the addition of yellow pigment; it was discovered when red fish yielded yellow offspring. One nonred mutation is dominant and another is recessive to normal red. Again, we may be dealing with at least two alleles and perhaps additional genes affecting red color.

The *black* bettas are the result of high concentrations of melanin (or possibly black pterin) pigment. There are several strains differing in intensity of color. In one strain the homozygous condition (black · black) is lethal so we don't know what it would look like were it to survive. All surviving black bettas of this strain are heterozygotes produced by crossing black fish with a blue fish. There is also a smoky black strain in which homozygotes survive. The genetics have not been worked out. Another kind of black, really a charcoal brown at best, breeds true but lacks intense blackness. It is likely that these fish are really pure black, but the final stage of the melanin polymer is reduced (brown) rather than oxidized (black). Perhaps some dietary oxidant that could find its way to the melanocyte might transform this fish to black.

Intensely black bettas are seldom seen in pet stores, but are available through IBC. The

Female marbled **Betta splendens.**

black gene suggests that bettas have an XX, XY chromosome system. We can get 100 percent fertile black males (XY) but 0 percent fertile black females (XX). That suggests that the gene for black is on a sex chromosome. The most intense black (called *melano*) interferes with reproductive success of females, so black bettas are usually maintained by breeding a black male with a steel blue female. That could lead to the inference that blue (GB), green (GG), steel blue (BB), and melano are all alleles, and that melano-melano is a lethal combination. Further, it suggests that the melano gene is on the X chromosome or its equivalent in bettas.

The marble betta looks like a mix of cambodia with a smattering of (usually) blue. It is a recessive trait, and can be written mbmb for the homozygous marble-appearing fish, ++ or MBMB for the non-marble wild type, or MBmb or +mb for the heterozygous yet normal-looking carrier of the marble gene.

We've discussed the genetics of green (GG), blue (GB), and steel blue (BB). The *quality* of green, blue, and steel blue bettas is influenced by the density of the underlying dermal pigments and the distribution, density and refraction of the crystalline guanine layers. See the box for more information.

The xanthic state is a yellow betta, and the yellow is visible because no other colors exist to block it. Yellow phenotypes appear in the absence of masking colors. Xanthic cambodia bettas can result either from interruption in melanin formation to stop at yellow or from a predominance of yellow xanthin pigments not masked by stronger colors. They might also be caused by yellow pterins. Note that red pigment in some bettas is produced by astaxanthin, and in other bettas by red

pterins. Crossing one red (or yellow) strain with another based on a different set of alleles can result in no red or yellow fish at all, but only regeneration of the wild dark betta. The best xanthic and cambodia bettas have pterin, xanthin, and other pigments controlled by the gene *nonred* that codes for an interrupted red pigment pathway that ends in yellow pigment on the body, but the complete pathway in the fins leading to a final red pigment.

Some *white cambodia* bettas appear to be semi-albinos in which all melanins, xanthins, and pterins are absent from the body and fins, but melanin pigment is retained in the eyes. Other cambodia strains have red, nonred or yellow pigments in the fins, and still other strains have colorless fins. Cambodia is symbolized with a small letter c, to indicate that it is recessive to the wild type, written C or +. A cambodia can only have the genotype cc, as the heterozygote (Cc or +c)

Gold butterfly twin tail **Betta splendens.**

would be pigmented on the body. Cambodia that produce offspring in ratios inconsistent with a single gene mutation (c) are probably multiple mutations for nonred (yellow) from both a pterin pathway and a xanthin pathway.

You can handle two sets of genes using Punnet Squares, and even more when you become comfortable with the technique. It's just a matter of starting with all possible combinations of genes in the chromosomes of the parents.

As an example let's start out knowing that long-fin is dominant to shortfin, and cornflower blue is an incomplete dominant of green and steel blue.

(homozygous longfin green male)

		LG	LG
(homozygous shortfin steel blue female)	IB	LIGB	LIGB
	IB	LIGB	LIGB

The offspring are all heterozygous long-finned and heterozygous cornflower blue. Now let's breed brother to sister. Each sperm and each egg can have any combination of fin length gene and either the green or blue gene.

	LG	LB	IG	IB
LG	LLGG	LLGB	LIGG	LIGB
LB	LLGB	LLBB	LIGB	LIBB
IG	LIGG	LIGB	IIGG	IIGB
IB	LIGB	LIBB	IIGB	IIBB

Now we have 16 possible combinations (four times four). Phenotypically we will have 75 percent long-finned and 25 percent short-finned fish. You can figure the percentages of green, steel blue, and cornflower blue fish, and the percentages of each color form with each fin type. A reminder—these are predicted ratios based on raising a large number of offspring, so the actual numbers will vary.

The genetics of colors and fins is still being worked out for *Betta splendens*, and isn't known for any other *Betta* species.

Green, Blue, and Steel Blue

What do the genes for green, steel blue, or deep cornflower blue control? Damselfish (*Chrysiptera cyanea*) can rapidly change from violet to blue or green because they have motile iridophores that alter their distance from underlying melanophores and from each other. Colors also depend on whether the melanosomes are expanded (dispersed) or contracted. The distance of the iridophore's guanine crystals from one another and from the dispersed or contracted melanophores changes the refraction of light. When light is refracted to emit at 532 nanometers, the fish appear green, but if it shifts to 485 nm, the fish is blue (Oshima et al., 1985; Fujii and Oshima, 1986; Kasukawa et al., 1986). In damselfish, hormone release rapidly determines the color of the moment. The same basic color system may occur in bettas, but the colors in bettas might be fixed because the iridophores are not motile and the melanosomes cannot disperse and contract.

The two most important sources of fancy domestic bettas and of wild bettas in the United States are the Aquabid Web site (www.aquabid.com) and the International Betta Congress (IBC).

Information and Sources of Fishes

Aquabid's listings change daily as breeders, collectors, and other suppliers around the globe offer show-quality and fighting-quality wild bettas from selectively bred strains at auction or at fixed rates. Malaysian and Indonesian collectors and transporters ship wild fish from originating locations to aquarists anywhere in the world using trans-shippers who deal with import regulations, change water in the bags, and re-ship the fish to the ultimate recipient. Domestic fancy betta breeders also advertise top quality show fish on Aquabid, which organizes offerings by fancy strain. Aquabid's options to sell fish at fixed prices or at auction make this site invaluable, providing everyone everywhere the same opportunities to acquire wonderful fish and, in turn, distribute offspring. Your best guide to the most reliable suppliers is the number and frequency of their listings and how long they have been providing services.

International Betta Congress

The International Betta Congress has members throughout the world. Sanctioned shows adhering to judging standards are held several times a year in the USA and Canada. The turn-out of aquarists (not only Betta keepers) in regional and national shows is impressive, and the forums are opportunities for experts and amateurs to learn from each other. The IBC

Betta Club Web Sites

International Betta Congress	*http://ibcbettas.org*
Anabantoid Association of Great Britain	*http://www.cfkc.demon.co.uk/club/aagb.htm*
European Anabantoid Club	*http://aklabyrinthfische-eac.eu*
German Anabantoid Club	*http://igl-home.de*
French Anabantoid Club	*http://cil.france.free.fr*
Malaysian Betta Club	*http://jyliew.tripod.com/index1.html*
Fish Hunters Team Borneo	*http://www5b.biglobe.ue.jp/~borneo/home.html*

also has a section devoted to the wild bettas and is an excellent source of new information and unusual species.

The major regional and local clubs are the Southern Betta Society, Everglades Betta Society, Aloha (Hawaii) Betta Chapter, Betta Association of the Southeast, Betta Buffs of Pittsburgh, California Betta Society, Philadelphia Area Betta Society, Hampton Roads (Virginia) Betta Breeders, Jersey Betta Breeders, Lone Star Bettas, Mid-Atlantic Organized Betta Breeders, Southern California Betta Club, and the Texas Area Betta Society. You can link to them all through the IBC's web site.

IBC publishes the quarterly journal FLARE, featuring innovations, reviews of techniques and standards, and explanations of genetics, nutrition, physiology, coloration, and other biological aspects of *Betta splendens*. IBC provides back issues of reports on genetics, colors, nutrition, judging, and other subjects. Back issues of FLARE and specific articles (or entire categories of articles) can be ordered for the cost of photocopying and shipping.

New members are offered two pairs of quality bettas for the cost of shipping, a service that introduces novices to trading fish through the mail. Many members sell fancy and wild strains through the mail. Members have the opportunity to find all manner of finnage and color variations of *Betta splendens* never available in pet stores.

The IBC Stock Shop link includes fish for sale, for trade, and wanted to buy advertisements. The listings from all over the world change constantly. A separate list is published on the internet for other species of *Betta*. IBC also provides members web links to sources of domesticated and wild bettas.

You'll be surprised how much information is at your fingertips by punching into your computer the keyword "betta."

Anabantoid Association of Great Britain

The AAGB was started in 1981 for the study, breeding, and conservation of anabantoids (labyrinth fishes). Several anabantoids are endangered as a result of deforestation destroying their habitats, hence the AAGB's emphasis on conservation projects such as that for the Eastern Cape Rocky (*Sandelia bainsii*) in the Baaukraantz Reserve in South Africa. By encouraging breeding and maintenance of vulnerable anabantoids such as *Sandelia capensis* and *Malpalutta kretseri*, the AAGB makes desirable fish available to members and reduces commercial demand for wild fish. The association has members from the USA, Canada, Singapore, Malaysia, UK, and all other parts of Europe. It shares expertise and experiences, and all of the members learn from each other. The AAGB issues a a bimonthly magazine with news and pictures, reviews of member weekends and members' day events that include presentations, slide shows, auctions, and social events. See *www.aagb.org*.

Further Reading

Allen, J. M., and P. F. Nicoletto. 1997. Response of *Betta splendens* to computer animations of males with fins of different length. Copeia **1997**(1):195–199.

Bagnara, J. T., J. Matsumoto, W. Ferris, S. K., Frost, W. A. Turner, Jr., and J. D. Taylor. 1979.

Two males exhibiting typical **Betta** *behavior.*

Common origin of pigment cells. Science **203**(4379):410–415.

Britz, R., M. Kokoscha, and R. Riehl. 1995. The anabantoid genera *Ctenops*, *Luciocephalus*, *Parasphaerichthys*, and *Sphaerichthys* (Teleostei: Perciformes) as a monophyletic group:

evidence from egg surface structure and reproductive behaviour. Japanese Journal of Ichthyology **42**(1):71–79.

Cole, B., C. S. Tamaru, R. Bailey, and C. Brown. 1997. A manual for commercial production of the gourami, *Trichogaster trichopterus*, a

Betta cf. unimaculata *new variation from Malek (male).*

temporary paired spawner. Center for Tropical and Subtropical Aquaculture Publication Number 135, 40 pp.

Degani, G. 1990. Effect of different diets and water quality on the growth of the larvae of *Trichogaster trichopterus* (B&S 1801). Aquacultural Engineering **9**:367–375.

Donoso, R. 1989. Further notes on *Betta coccina*. Labyrinth, newsletter no. 42, February, 3–9.

Fujii, R., and N. Oshima. 1986. Control of chromatophore movements in teleost fishes. Zoological Science **3**:13–17.

Hisaoka, K. K., and C. F. Firlit. 1963. The embryology of the blue gourami, *Trichogaster trichopterus*. Journal of Morphology **111**:239–243.

Goldstein, R. J. 1971. *Anabantoids. Gouramies and Related Fishes.* T.F.H. Publications, Jersey City, NJ, 160 pp.

Goldstein, R. J., C. Hopper and G. Pottern. 2000. Report of a chloramine fish kill. Southeastern Society of Parasitologists annual meeting, Chattanooga, TN, abstract.

Kottelat, M. 1994. Diagnoses of two new species of fighting fishes from Thailand and Cambodia (Teleostei: Belontiidae). Ichthyological Exploration of Freshwaters **5**(4):297–304.

Linke, H. 1989. *Betta* foerschi - Schaumnesterbauer oder Maulbruter? Der Makropode **10**(3):34–36.

Linke, H. 1991. *Labyrinth Fish, The Bubble-Nest-Builders*, Tetra (Division of Warner-Lambert), Morris Plains, NJ, 174 pp.

Lucas, G. 1983. On sex reversal in *Betta splendens*: is sex ever a sure thing? Freshwater and Marine Aquarium **6**(1):26–28, 70–75.

Ng, P. K. L. 1993. On a new species of *Betta* (Teleostei: Belontiidae) from peat swamps in Sabah, East Malaysia, Borneo. Ichthyological Exploration of Freshwaters 4(4):289–294.

Ng, P. K. L., and M. Kottelat. 1992. *Betta livida*, a new fighting fish (Teleostei: Belontiidae) from blackwater swamps in peninsular Malaysia. Ichthyological Exploration of Freshwaters 3(2):177–182.

Pinter, H. 1984. *Labyrinth Fish*. Barron's Educational Series, Inc., Hauppauge, NY, 144 pp.

Pinto, T. 1999. *Betta dimidiata* - luck the second time around. Belontid 1(1):3–5.

Richter, H-J. 1983. *Das Buch der Labyrinthfische*. Verlag J. Neumann-Neudamm, Berlin, 167 pp.

Royal, B. K., and G. A. Lucas. 1972–1973. Analysis of red and yellow pigments in two mutants of the Siamese fighting fish, *Betta splendens*. Proceedings of the Iowa Academy of Sciences 79(1972–1973):34–37.

Schindler, I., and J. Schmidt. 2004. *Betta pallida* spec. nov., a new fighting fish from southern Thailand (Teleostei: Belontiidae). Zeitschrift fur Fischkunde 7(1): 1–4.

Schindler, I., and J. Schmidt. 2006. Review of the mouthbrooding *Betta* (Teleostei, Osphronemidae) from Thailand, with descriptions of two new species. Zeitschrift fur Fischkunde 8(1,2): 47–69.

Schindler, I., and J. Schmidt. 2008. *Betta kuehnei*, a new species of fighting fish (Teleostei, Osphronemidae) from the Malay Peninsula. Bulletin of Fish Biology 10(1,2): 39–46.

Tan, H.H. 2009. *Betta pardalotos*, a new species of fighting fish (Teleostei: Osphronemidae) from Sumatra, Indonesia. The Raffles Museum of Zoology 57(2):501–504.

Tan, H.H. 2009. Redescription of *Betta anabatoides* Bleeker, and a new species of *Betta* from West Kalimantan, Borneo (Teleostei: Osphronemidae). Zootaxa 2165: 59–68.

Tan, H.H., and K.K. P. Lim. 2004. Inland fishes from the Anambas and Natuna islands, South China Sea, with description of a new species of *Betta* (Teleostei: Osphronemidae). Raffles Bulletin of Zoology Supplement 11:107–115.

Tan, H. H., and M. Kottelat. 1998a. Two new species of *Betta* (Teleostei: Osphronemidae) from the Kapuas basin, Kalimantan Barat, Borneo. Raffles Bulletin of Zoology 46(1): 41–51.

Tan, H. H., and M. Kottelat. 1998b. Redescription of *Betta picta* (Teleostei: Osphronemidae) and description of *B. falx* sp.n. from central Sumatra. Revue Suisse de Zoologie 105(3):557–568.

Tan, H.H., and P.K.L. Ng. 2005. The labyrinth fishes (Teleostei: Anabantoidei, Channoidei) of Sumatra, Indonesia. Raffles Bulletin of Zoology, Supplement 13:115–138.

Tan, H., and P.K.L. Ng. 2006. Six new species of fighting fish (Teleostei: Osphronemidae: *Betta*) from Borneo. Ichthyological Exploration of Freshwaters 17(2):97–114.

Tan, H. H., and P. K. L. Ng. 1996. Redescription of *Betta bellica* Sauvage, 1884, with description of a new allied species from Sumatra. Raffles Bulletin of Zoology 44(1):143–155.

Witte, K., and J. Schmidt. 1992. *Betta brownorum*, a new species of anabantoids (Teleostei: Belontiidae) from northwestern Borneo, with a key to the genus. Ichthyological Exploration of Freshwaters 2(4):305–330.

I N D E X

Acknowledgments

Many individuals provided the fishes, photographs, technical reports, journals, experiences, and criticism. They deserve to be considered coauthors.

David Armitage of the British wild betta group provided narratives of expeditions to Asia taken with Tony Pinto of Massachusetts, photographs of wild bettas and habitats, and reviewed the text. William Bavier of Fort Lauderdale showed me around his enormous breeding facilities and described how he produces show quality fish. George Benz of the Tennessee Aquarium provided information on parasites of anabantoids. Ralf Britz of Germany sent scientific research explaining the latest family classification. Philippe Chevoleau of France introduced me to the French anabantoid society and its publications. Alejandro Farrell of Argentina led me to Asian bulletin board sites frequented by experts unknown in this country. Yohan Fernando of Illinois offered insights into the IBC, wild betta care, and reviewed the entire text. Marleen Janson of Wisconsin tracked down great leads and a photographer. Gilbert Limhengco of California sent wild and show bettas to breed and photograph, and offered tips on handling species new to me. Ed Lines of the Shedd Aquarium provided photos of Marleen Janson's bettas. Peter Liptrot of the UK provided photos and breeding information for *Betta rubra*. Gene Lucas of Iowa critically reviewed the sections on genetics and pigments through several iterations. Robert Nhan of California steered me to other experts listed here I would not have met otherwise. Tony Pinto of Massachusetts provided rare species for breeding and photography, distributional reports based on his collecting trips to Asia, and breeding reports from his own tanks and from the German literature. Tan Hoek Hui of Singapore critically reviewed the manuscript of the first edition for technical accuracy, offered many helpful suggestions and corrections to the taxonomic and distributional information, sent research papers on wild bettas, graphics from his reports describing differences within species groups, and provided photographs of many species of wild bettas. Anuratana (Tony) Tejavej of Bangkok reviewed and improved the manuscript, supplied photographs of Thai fighting fish markets, and sent wild bettas all the way from Thailand. K.A. Webb took many photos sent by David Armitage. Marc Weiss of Fort Lauderdale handled the importation from Thailand, loaned his complete set of *Ichthyological Explorations of Freshwaters*, corrected the text, ferried me to expert betta breeders, and explained the business of collecting and importing domestic and wild bettas from Asia. Todd Wenzel of North Carolina provided boxes of back issues of commercial and local society periodicals. A special thanks to Colin Dunlop, Jens Kuehne, Michael Lo, Oliver Lucanus, Anthony Terceira, Stefan van der Voort, and K. A. Webb for their photos for the second edition, and to Marcy Rosenbaum, my editor at Barron's, for bringing order to my chaos and designing a beautiful book.

—Robert J. Goldstein, October 2011.

Cover Photos

Shutterstock: front cover, back cover, inside front cover, inside back cover.

Photo Credits

Cecilia Bailey: page 80; Colin Dunlop: pages 22, 55, (top right), 60 (top left), 61 (top); Robert J. Goldstein: page 79; Dan H. Johnson, D.V.M.: page 81; Daniel Johnson/Paulette Johnson: page 68; Jens Kuehne Photography: pages 11, 14, 51 (bottom), 52 (bottom), 53 (top right), 65; Michael Lo: pages 29, 30 (top), 33, 36 (top right), 37, 41, 47, 49 (top), 51 (top), 52 (top), 53 (top right), 54 (bottom), 55 (bottom), 56, 57 (top); Oliver Lucanus: pages 12, 13, 26 (top), 27 (top), 31, 32, 35, 36 (center left), 36 (center right), 36 (bottom right), 40, 42 (top), 43, 45 (top), 46 (top), 46 (bottom), 48 (top), 48 (bottom), 50, 54 (top), 57 (bottom), 59, 60 (bottom), 61 (bottom), 77, 86, 93, 100, 105; Helen E. Roberts, D.V.M.: page 82; Shutterstock: pages 2, 8 (all, except bottom left), 9 (all, except top right), 67, 83; Anthony C. Terceira: pages 4, 5, 7, 8 (bottom left), 18, 19, 20, 21, 24, 27 (bottom), 28 (top), 28 (bottom), 30 (bottom), 34 (top), 34 (bottom), 36 (top left), 36 (bottom left), 39, 69, 70, 71, 72 (top), 72 (bottom), 74, 75, 76, 84, 85, 88, 92, 96, 97, 104, 107; Stefan van der Voort: pages 25 (top), 26 (bottom), 38, 44 (bottom), 45 (bottom), 53 (bottom), 55 (top left), 58, 60 (top right), 64, 73, 108; K. A. Webb: pages 9 (top right), 10, 17, 25 (bottom), 42 (bottom), 44 (top), 49 (bottom), 87 (top), 87 (bottom), 99, 101, 102.

All inquiries should be addressed to:
Barron's Educational Series, Inc.
250 Wireless Boulevard
Hauppauge, NY 11788
www.barronseduc.com

ISBN: 978-0-7641-4742-5
Library of Congress Catalog Card No. 2011941458

Printed in China
9 8 7 6 5 4 3 2 1